A Study of Key Terms in Article 82 of the United Nations Convention on the Law of the Sea

ISA TECHNICAL STUDY: NO. 15

ISA Technical Study Series

Technical Study No. 1
Global Non-Living Resources on the Extended Continental Shelf:
Prospects at the Year 2000

Technical Study No. 2
Polymetallic Massive Sulphides and Cobalt-Rich Ferromanganese Crusts:
Status and Prospects

Technical Study No. 3
Biodiversity, Species Ranges and Gene Flow in the Abyssal Pacific Nodule
Province: Predicting and Managing the Impacts of Deep Seabed Mining

Technical Study No. 4
Issues associated with the Implementation of Article 82 of the United
Nations Convention on the Law of the Sea

Technical Study No. 5
Non-Living Resources of the Continental Shelf Beyond 200 Nautical Miles:
Speculations on the Implementation of Article 82 of the United
Nations Convention on the Law of the Sea

Technical Study No. 6
A Geological Model of Polymetallic Nodule Deposits in the
Clarion-Clipperton Fracture Zone

Technical Study No. 7
Marine Benthic Nematode Molecular Protocol Handbook – Nematode Barcoding

Technical Study No. 8
Fauna of Cobalt-Rich Ferromanganese Crust Seamounts

Technical Study No. 9
Environmental Management of Deep-Sea Chemosynthetic Ecosystems:
Justification of and Considerations for a Spatially-Based Approach

Technical Study No. 10
Environmental Management Needs for Exploration and
Exploitation of Deep Sea Minerals

Technical Study No. 11
Towards the Development of a Regulatory Framework
for Polymetallic Nodule Exploitation in the Area

Technical Study No. 12
Implementation of Article 82 of the United Nations
Convention on the Law of the Sea

Technical Study No: 13
Deep Sea Macrofauna of the Clarion-Clipperton Zone: Taxonomic
Standardization Workshop, Republic of Korea, 2014

Technical Study No. 14
Submarine Cables and Deep Seabed Mining

A Study of Key Terms in Article 82 of the United Nations Convention on the Law of the Sea

ISA TECHNICAL STUDY: NO. 15

Authored By:
Wylie Spicer, Q.C.
Elizabeth McIsaac

*With thanks to Rohan Rajpal, an articling clerk with McInnes Cooper
for his assistance in preparing this report*

International Seabed Authority
Kingston, Jamaica

NATIONAL LIBRARY OF JAMAICA CATALOGUING-IN-PUBLICATION DATA

Spicer , Wylie
    A study of key terms in Article 82 of the United Nations Convention on the Law of the Sea / by Wylie Spicer, Elizabeth McIsaac.

    p. ; cm – (ISA technical study; no. 15)
ISBN 978-976-8241-41-2(pbk)
ISBN 978-976-8241-42-9 (ebk)

1. Law of the Sea   2.   Maritime law – International cooperation
3. Ocean bottom – Law and legislation – International cooperation
I. McIsaac, Elizabeth   II. Title   III. Series

341.450268 dc 23

Table of Contents

Foreword

Article 82 of the United Nations Convention on the Law of the Sea provides for a system of payments and contributions by coastal States with respect to the exploitation of non-living resources of the continental shelf beyond 200 nautical miles from the baseline (sometimes referred to as the 'outer continental shelf' or 'extended continental shelf'). Paragraph 4 of Article 82 requires that the payments or contributions are to be made through the International Seabed Authority for distribution to States Parties to the Convention.

Although brief, consisting of only four short paragraphs, Article 82 is in fact a very complex provision. In understanding how to implement its provisions, consideration will need to be given to the legal nature of the obligations established by Article 82, the principles and criteria for distribution of benefits, procedural aspects, the role of the Authority, the role of 'OCS States' and other economic and temporal issues.

With a view to preparing for the discharge of its responsibilities in this respect, in 2009 the Authority convened a seminar to discuss the issues associated with Article 82, in conjunction with the Royal Institute of International Affairs (Chatham House) in the United Kingdom. Two ISA technical studies (No. 4 and No. 5) were issued following the seminar. One of the key conclusions of the seminar was that Article 82 has several textual ambiguities and gaps raising questions that require clarification.

As a follow-up to the Chatham House seminar, an international workshop was held in 2012 at Beijing, China, with the aim of drawing up guidelines for the implementation of Article 82 and the outlines of a model agreement between the Authority and an OCS State for receiving payments and distribution. The workshop noted that Article 82 does not provide definitions for many of the key terms used, in particular 'resource', 'all production', 'value', 'volume', 'site', 'payments', 'contribution in kind' and 'annually'. Each term would require individual clarification, with reference to the use of other terms, to correctly and fairly reflect the intention behind the whole provision and in the context of the Convention, and in order to promote uniformity in State practice. It was also noted that in different OCS States some of these terms may not be understood in the same manner or might no longer be in use as a result of departure from royalty-based approaches to determining a government's share of produced resources to other forms of revenue-sharing. While a measure of flexibility of interpretation in particular cases might be desirable, the terms also represent common denominators for all OCS States for the implementation of Article 82. Therefore, consistent understanding among States Parties would facilitate implementation and avoid potential disputes regarding interpretation. The workshop felt that a clear and common understanding of the terminology, and especially the functions performed by those terms in the contemporary context of Article 82, required further expert input, which could be in the form of a study of the use of those terms internationally. The workshop therefore recommended that further examination of the implementation needs of Article 82 would benefit from a study of the key terms used in Article 82 and implicit from its context as used in contemporary and industry practices across different jurisdictions. The study would help identify possible paths for a practical approach and build and deepen understanding of the terminological issues in realistic settings.

The present technical study is issued in response to that recommendation. Research was carried out between October 2015 and March 2016. Since there are currently no mineral resource operations taking place beyond 200 nautical miles on the continental shelf or in the Area, this study of key terms used in Article 82 is mainly restricted to the consideration of hydrocarbons. While domestic legislation with respect to royalties and taxation of petroleum resources is not prescriptive with respect to the implementation of an international treaty, such legislation is informative with respect to many of the legal and administrative issues that may be relevant for the implementation of Article 82. In this study, nine jurisdictions were reviewed for their relevant Article 82 terms.

It is hoped that this technical study will be useful to States Parties in broadening their understanding of key terms used in Article 82 and will also contribute to further discussions within the Authority on practical measures for implementation of its responsibilities under Article 82.

Kingston, June 2016

Michael W. Lodge
Deputy to the Secretary-General and Legal Counsel
International Seabed Authority

Terms of Reference

McInnes Cooper was retained by the International Seabed Authority to conduct a study of key terms in Article 82 of the United Nations Convention on the Law of the Sea ("UNCLOS").

This study was to consider both "hydrocarbons" and "mineral resources" consistent with the terms of Article 82.

There are currently no mineral resource operations taking place beyond 200 nautical miles on the continental shelf or pursuant to Part XI of UNCLOS. More generally, there are no substantive data in respect of mineral resources to provide a comparative base for Article 82.

The accompanying study of key terms in Article 82 is restricted to the consideration of hydrocarbons.

Introduction

Article 82 of UNCLOS requires its signatories to make payments in respect of exploitation of the continental shelf beyond 200 nautical miles. This Article has been viewed as dormant, but recent developments in offshore exploration have provided motivation for the development of an interpretive framework for this Article. Such a framework will enable the orderly administration of required payments to the International Seabed Authority (the Authority). Article 82 reads as follows:

Article 82

Payments and contributions with respect to the exploitation of the continental shelf beyond 200 nautical miles

1. The coastal State shall make payments or contributions in kind in respect of the exploitation of the non-living resources of the continental shelf beyond 200 nautical miles from the baselines from which the breadth of the territorial sea is measured.

2. The payments and contributions shall be made annually with respect to all production at a site after the first five years of production at that site. For the sixth year, the rate of payment or contribution shall be 1 per cent of the value or volume of production at the site. The rate shall increase by 1 per cent for each subsequent year until the twelfth year and shall remain at 7 per cent thereafter. Production does not include resources used in connection with exploitation.

3. A developing State which is a net importer of a mineral resource produced from its continental shelf is exempt from making such payments or contributions in respect of that mineral resource.

4. The payments or contributions shall be made through the Authority, which shall distribute them to States Parties to this Convention, on the basis of equitable sharing criteria, taking into account the interests and needs of developing States, particularly the least developed and the land-locked among them.

Commentators have stated that the language used in Article 82 is ambiguous. In particular, the terms "resource", "all production", "value", "volume", "site, "payments", "contribution in kind" and "annually" may be subject to different interpretations. Academic commentators have raised the following interpretive questions with respect to these terms:

Term	Issue
Resource	Are resources processed or raw? Are "derived commodities" resources? At what point in time is the resource measured for royalty calculation (*e.g.* extraction, sale)? At what location is value/volume calculated?
All Production/Volume	Does "all production" mean gross or net production? Are any volume deductions permitted? What does it mean for resources to be used in connection with exploitation?
Value	How is "all production" or "volume" valued? Are any financial deductions allowed (*e.g.* expense/risk of deep water drilling, transportation, processing)? Are regional markets or transportation taken into account?
Contributions in kind	How are contributions in kind administered? At what point does legal title to the production pass? Who bears related costs to contributions in kind (*e.g.* storage, transportation)?
Site	On what area is the royalty or tax payable (resource field, geologic structure, well site, license area, project)? How are transboundary resources addressed? How is unitization addressed?
Payments	In what currency should payments be made? How should currency conversions be performed?
Annually	What is the periodicity of payments?

Academic commentators and participants in workshops held by the Authority have provided normative interpretations of these terms.[1] The consensus is that the attributions of meaning set out below are appropriate for Article 82:

---

[1] Wylie Spicer, "Canada, the Law of the Sea Treaty and International Payments: Where Will the Money Come From?" (2015) 8:31 University of Calgary SPP Research Papers; International Seabed Authority, "Implementation of Article 82 of the United Nations Convention on the Law of the Sea: ISA Technical Study No. 12" (Kingston, Jamaica: 2012) at 19-22, containing Aldo Chircop, "Development of Guidelines for the Implementation of Article 82 (Working Paper)" at 47-52; International Seabed

Term	Issue
Resource	• Non-living (*i.e.* minerals and hydrocarbons). • Product to be ready for market distribution or processing.
All Production/Volume	• Gross, not net, of commercial production. • Determined at wellhead. • Commercial production to exclude test production. • Reinjected and flared gas excluded from calculation. • No deduction of financial resources.
Value	• Directly linked to "all production". • Based on gross production and fair market value at wellhead. • No deduction of cost elements before value/volume determined. • Value and volume calculations should produce the same result. • Method of calculation should be disclosed.
Contributions in kind	• No substantial difference in discharging obligation through value or contribution in kind.
Site	• Geographic location of a resource. • May be a delineated field or a site as defined by the state.
Payments	• Payment in convertible currency and regular schedules of payments preferable.
Annually	• No consensus on whether this is a financial or calendar year. • Possibly a scheme of transfers spread throughout the year.

In addition to expert interpretation regarding the attribution of the Article 82 terms, other interpretive sources are relevant. In particular, the current use of these terms and concepts in the legislation of various petroleum producing states is informative in determining the common meaning of the terms in question. While domestic legislation with respect to royalties and taxation of petroleum resources is not prescriptive with respect to the interpretation of an international treaty, such legislation is informative with respect to legal and administrative issues that may be relevant for the implementation of Article 82.

In total, nine jurisdictions were reviewed for their legislative use of the relevant Article 82 terms: the United States of America, Brazil, Alberta (Canada), Newfoundland and Labrador (Canada), Australia (Commonwealth), Nigeria, the Russian Federation, the United Kingdom, and Norway.

Authority, "Issues Associated with the Implementation of Article 82 of the United Nations Convention on the Law of the Sea: Technical Study No. 4" (Kingston, Jamaica: 2009) at 31-34.

Executive Summary

In general, the "resource" that is subject to taxation or royalty payment is the raw resource and not a derived commodity. Nonetheless, several jurisdictions either require or accommodate valuation at a point in the extraction process where hydrocarbons have received some initial treatment. For example, the United States requires that the product be placed in "marketable condition" before it is valued. Russia charges its extraction tax with respect to oil that has been dewatered, desalted, and stabilized. In the United Kingdom, certain resource values are calculated on the assumption that the resource has undergone appropriate initial treatment. In this context, initial treatment includes the separation of oil and gas, the liquefying of gas for transportation, as well as other processes that enable the hydrocarbon to be safely stored, loaded into a tanker, or accepted by an oil refinery. Initial treatment does not include refining or deballasting.

A notable exception to the general practice of valuing raw resources for royalty calculation purposes is the valuation of processed gas. The United States and Alberta provide mechanisms for valuing both processed and unprocessed gas. Nonetheless, since processing costs are generally deductible in these jurisdictions, there is effectively no royalty on the added value of processing. In other words, by permitting processed gas to be valued but deducting the expense of processing, the royalty is closely related to the value of the raw resource.

The production volume used to calculate the royalty is generally subject to a number of deductions. Reasonable losses, unavoidable losses, or losses up to a certain prescribed limit are generally not subject to royalty (as in USA, Australia, Russia, UK, Nigeria). Further, most jurisdictions provide for the deduction of certain flared or reinjected gas.

Certain hydrocarbons used for production purposes are deductible in most jurisdictions (*e.g.* USA, UK, Australia, Alberta, Nigeria) but not in others (*e.g.* Brazil). Production purposes may include drilling for resources, gathering resources on a lease, pumping resources onshore, and subjecting the resource to initial treatment, or the operation of gas processing plants.

Notably, Brazil requires royalty payments for test production if the resource is used economically. Conversely, the United States has indicated in its recent calls for bids for offshore leases that commercial production does not include test production. Newfoundland and Labrador has statutory provisions requiring royalty payments for flow testing.

There is considerable variation between jurisdictions regarding the appropriate mechanism to value the production volume on which royalty is payable. What the regimes have in common is that the mechanism is designed to approximate the market value of the production volume. This may be achieved by considering the actual sale price of the resource, or by calculating a price for the resource using the market value or a value ascribed by the regulator. A primary consideration for determining whether a resource sale price is an appropriate value for tax or royalty purposes is whether the sale contract was made between affiliated parties (*i.e.* a non-arm's length contract).

A common feature of the various valuation mechanisms is the design which facilitates a consistent value of production regardless of additional services that may be provided incidental to the sale or disposition of the resource. As stated above, in jurisdictions that provide a mechanism for valuing processed gas, processing costs are generally deductible.

Similarly, most jurisdictions allow for adjustments in respect of transportation costs when determining the royalty or tax payment (e.g. Alberta, USA, Brazil, Russia, Newfoundland and Labrador, Nigeria). In effect, this means that royalty is not generally payable on the portion of the sale price that is earned for transportation services. Alternatively, in the United Kingdom, which taxes offshore profits instead of charging a royalty on production, transportation costs are ascribed to certain transactions regardless of what transportation costs are actually incurred, which results in a consistent treatment of this source of revenue. Norway also has a pricing mechanism that accounts for transportation costs.

Generally, financial resources other than those used for processing and transportation are not deductible with respect to royalty payments on produced resources. Nonetheless, financial resources including operating and capital costs may be deductible where the jurisdiction requires payments in respect of profits earned. This is the case in Norway and the United Kingdom, which have profit taxation systems. Further, Brazil requires payments for "special participation" (separate from royalty) in circumstances where there are large production volumes or high profitability. This special participation is payable on gross production revenue less the value of royalties paid by the producer, production investments, operational costs, depreciation, and taxes. Similar "tiered" royalty payments, above and beyond basic royalty, are payable in Newfoundland and Labrador.

There is considerable variation in royalty rates between jurisdictions. Royalties in the jurisdictions reviewed are not generally payable at a flat rate. Instead the rate is adjusted to compensate for factors that influence the expense or risk of producing the resource, or to incentivize certain types of production. Further, royalty relief is available in many jurisdictions as an additional incentive for certain types of production.

Most jurisdictions do not have statutory provisions regarding royalties in kind. Those jurisdictions that do have laws on royalties in kind (i.e. United States, Alberta, Newfoundland and Labrador) generally allow a producer to deduct transportation expenses. This is consistent with the treatment of transportation expenses where the royalty is due in value instead of in kind.

Newfoundland and Labrador provides detailed regulatory provisions on contributions in kind. Under these regulations, the government may require oil taken in kind to be delivered at a loading point (i.e. the final point of measurement of the production facilities of a lease prior to the loading of oil for transportation), the place where title passes to an arm's length purchaser, the entry valve of a refinery, or at a transshipment facility. Further, an interest holder may be required to take, transport, transship and store the oil that is being taken in kind for the government. Nonetheless, where an interest holder provides storage and transportation for oil taken in kind, the government will pay for these services as set out in the regulation. Notably, risk remains with the interest holder until the oil is delivered in the manner requested by the government.

The nine jurisdictions reviewed were generally inconsistent with respect to the terms "site", "payment", and "annually". Depending on the jurisdiction, "site" could mean the lease, well, field, unit, or project area. In Norway, there is a single offshore area for taxation.

Most jurisdictions require "payment" in domestic currency. Russia and Brazil provide concrete guidance on how currency conversions may be performed. Nonetheless, the preference for domestic currency means the legislation reviewed is of limited use for determining the appropriate currency for an international administrative regime.

Finally, most jurisdictions have a tax or royalty assessment period that is shorter than "annually". While relevant annual periods generally refer to a calendar year, the legislation reviewed has limited use for determining the meaning of this term.

PART 1 : ROYALTY REGIME

UNITED STATES OF AMERICA

Resource	The lessee is required to put oil and gas in marketable condition at no cost to the government. There are no standards for valuing processed oil, but there are separate standards for the valuation of processed and unprocessed gas. Generally, quantity and quality of oil and unprocessed gas are determined at a point of royalty settlement approved by the responsible government authority. If processed gas is being valued, the quantity is determined by the net output of the processing plant.
All Production/Volume	Royalty is not payable on resources that are unavoidably lost or used on or for the benefit of the lease (which may include off-lease uses). Royalty is not payable for certain gas plant products that are reinjected into a reservoir or used to operate a processing plant. It is not likely that royalty will be payable on test production.
Value	Value depends on whether production is disposed of through an arm's length or non-arm's length contract, and for gas, whether it is processed or unprocessed. Under arm's length sales, value is generally equal to "gross proceeds" from the sale. Value for non-arm's length sales is calculated to approximate market value. Applicable deductions may include transportation and gas processing costs. There are no deductions for marketing or putting the product in marketable condition. Adjustments for quality and location differentials may be appropriate if value is calculated using market prices, or is related to an exchange agreement.
Site	The USA has defined "site" as an individual lease for the purposes of Article 82. The lease defines the area for which royalties are payable, though regulations on royalty relief set out complex rules on determining the area for which royalty relief may be applicable. Depending on the type of lease, royalties may be suspended on the basis of geologic fields, lease areas, project areas, or particular wells.
Payments	Valuation in foreign currency is not contemplated.
Contributions in kind	The royalty is to be paid in value unless the Office of Natural Resources Revenue requires payment in kind. Lessee is required to put royalty production into marketable condition at no cost to government. If the lessee processes royalty gas or delivers royalty oil or gas at a point not on or adjacent to the lease, a processing or transportation deduction may be available. The "Royalty-in-Kind Programme" is now closed.
Annually	Royalty is payable monthly.

Introduction

Title 30 of the Code of Federal Regulations (CFR) enables the federal government to collect royalties on federal oil and gas leases. This includes the valuation of oil[2] and gas[3] royalties for onshore leases and leases located on the Outer Continental Shelf, which is given a broad definition under the CFR:

> *Outer Continental Shelf (OCS)* means all submerged lands lying seaward and outside of the area of lands beneath navigable waters as defined in Section 2 of the Submerged Lands Act (43 U.S.C. 1301) and of which the subsoil and seabed appertain to the United States and are subject to its jurisdiction and control.[4]

The USA has formally addressed Article 82 requirements in its calls for bids, setting out the circumstances under which a lessee may be responsible for making UNCLOS related royalty payments.[5] Calls for bids have also defined how certain Article 82 terms should be interpreted. In particular, a "site" will be defined as an individual lease whether or not the lease is located in a unit. Further, the United States has indicated that "first production" begins on the first day of commercial production, excluding test production, which may assist in determining when the obligation to make royalty payments begins.

Title 30 of the CFR also sets out regulations for calculating royalties for Indian oil and gas leases and royalties for other types of resources. These regulations do not form part of this review.

Federal Oil Royalty

Resource, All Production, and Volume

Unlike federal gas royalties, reviewed later in this section, there is no mechanism in the CFR for valuing oil that has undergone processing. Instead, the quality and quantity of production for which royalties are payable is determined at a "point of settlement" for the lease, which is approved by the Bureau of Land Management ("BLM") for onshore leases or the Bureau of Safety and Environmental Enforcement ("BSEE") for offshore leases.[6]

Royalties are payable on 100 per cent of the volume measured at the point of settlement, and losses after this point will not result in a reduction in the royalty payment.[7] Royalties are not payable on unavoidable losses before the point of settlement,[8] although royalties are payable for wasted or avoidably lost oil.[9]

---

[2]   30 CFR §1206.100(a).
[3]   30 CFR §1206.150(a).
[4]   30 CFR §1206.101, §1206.151.
[5]   International Seabed Authority, "Issues Associated With the Implementation of Article 82 of the United Nations Convention on the Law of the Sea: Technical Study No. 4" (Kingston, Jamaica: 2009) at 5-8.
[6]   30 CFR §1206.119(a). Under §1206.119(b) a quantity/quality adjustment may be appropriate.
[7]   30 CFR §1206.119(d).
[8]   30 CFR §1206.119(c), 30 CFR §1202.100(b)(1).
[9]   30 CFR §1202.100(c).

The lessee is not required to pay a royalty for oil used on or for the benefit of the lease, including oil that is used off-lease for the benefit of the lease when such off-lease use is permitted by the responsible authority.[10]

Generally, financial resources used in connection with exploitation are not deductible when calculating royalty payments. For example, costs for gathering oil on a lease, putting oil in marketable condition, and marketing the oil are not deductible when calculating royalty payments.[11] Permissible deductions and allowances are discussed in the subsequent section on "value" and include certain transportation costs as well as adjustments for quality and location.

Value

Sale Type

The royalty payment is equal to the value of the production multiplied by the royalty rate set out in the lease.[12] The primary consideration in determining the value of the oil on which the lessee must pay a royalty is whether or not the oil was sold at arm's length, since the contract price of non-arm's length sales may not reflect the market price of the resource. Arm's length contracts are defined as follows:

> *Arm's-length contract* means a contract or agreement between independent persons who are not affiliates and who have opposing economic interests regarding that contract. To be considered arm's length for any production month, a contract must satisfy this definition for that month, as well as when the contract was executed.[13]

Arm's Length Sales

If oil is sold at arm's length, the value of the oil is equal to the "gross proceeds" accruing to the seller under the contract, less applicable allowances, which are reviewed in greater detail below.[14] *Gross proceeds* are defined as the total monies and other consideration accruing for the disposition of oil produced:

> *Gross proceeds* means the total monies and other consideration accruing for the disposition of oil produced. Gross proceeds also include, but are not limited to, the following examples:
>
> > (1) Payments for services such as dehydration, marketing, measurement, or gathering which the lessee must perform at no cost to the Federal Government;
> >
> > (2) The value of services, such as salt water disposal, that the producer normally performs but that the buyer performs on the producer's behalf;

---

[10]   30 CFR §1202.100(b)(1) (the responsible authority is Bureau of Ocean Energy Management, Regulation, and Enforcement or the Bureau of Land Management, depending on the lease type).

[11]   30 CFR §1206.106, 30 CFR §1206.101 ("gross proceeds").

[12]   30 CFR §1202.100(a).

[13]   30 CFR §1206.101.

[14]   30 CFR §1206.102.

(3) Reimbursements for harboring or terminaling fees;

(4) Tax reimbursements, even though the Federal royalty interest may be exempt from taxation;

(5) Payments made to reduce or buy down the purchase price of oil to be produced in later periods, by allocating such payments over the production whose price the payment reduces and including the allocated amounts as proceeds for the production as it occurs; and

(6) Monies and all other consideration to which a seller is contractually or legally entitled, but does not seek to collect through reasonable efforts.[15]

If gross proceeds accruing to the seller under an arm's length contract do not capture the reasonable value of the production, the lessee may be required to use the valuation mechanism set out for non-arm's length sales.[16]

Non-arm's Length Sales

Where oil is sold through a non-arm's length contract, value is calculated using a different mechanism.[17] The calculation of value depends on the geographic region in which the oil-producing lease is located.[18] The three general regions that are relevant under the valuation rules are California and Alaska,[19] the Rocky Mountain Region,[20] and locations other than California, Alaska, and the Rocky Mountain Region.[21] While there are several mechanisms available, generally, value may be calculated using market prices (*e.g.* NYMEX, ANS) with certain adjustments for location and quality differentials, and applicable transportation costs.[22]

Deductions and Allowances

Transportation Allowance

Royalty is generally not payable on proceeds that are attributable to the transportation of the resource. In the "value" determination, this is achieved through a deduction of the reasonable and actual costs of transporting oil from the lease to a point of sale off of the lease.[23] However, the transportation allowance may not exceed 50 per cent of the value of the oil.[24] "Transportation allowance" is defined as follows:

---

[15] 30 CFR §1206.101.
[16] 30 CFR §1206.102(c).
[17] 30 CFR §1206.103.
[18] 30 CFR §1206.103.
[19] 30 CFR §1206.103(a).
[20] 30 CFR §1206.103(b).
[21] 30 CFR §1206.103(c).
[22] 30 CFR §1206.103(a)(3), §1206.103(b)(3), §1206.103(c), §1206.112.
[23] 30 CFR §1206.109; see 30 CFR §1206.109-111 for more detail on the transportation allowance.
[24] 30 CFR §1206.109(c).

Transportation allowance means a deduction in determining royalty value for the reasonable, actual costs of moving oil to a point of sale or delivery off the lease, unit area, or communitized area. The transportation allowance does not include gathering costs.[25]

Gathering costs, defined as follows, are not deductible:

Gathering means the movement of lease production to a central accumulation or treatment point on the lease, unit, or communitized area, or to a central accumulation or treatment point off the lease, unit, or communitized area that BLM or BSEE approves for onshore and offshore leases, respectively.[26]

No Allowance for Marketing or Putting Oil in Marketable Condition

There is no allowance for the work or financial resources required to put the production into marketable condition, which is defined as follows:

Marketable condition means oil sufficiently free from impurities and otherwise in a condition a purchaser will accept under a sales contract typical for the field or area.[27]

Under the CFR, if the seller does not perform these services the value on which royalties are payable must be increased to compensate for these services:

You must place oil in marketable condition and market the oil for the mutual benefit of the lessee and the lessor at no cost to the Federal Government. If you use gross proceeds under an arm's-length contract in determining value, you must increase those gross proceeds to the extent that the purchaser, or any other person, provides certain services that the seller normally would be responsible to perform to place the oil in marketable condition or to market the oil.[28]

Quality and Location Adjustments

A value adjustment for quality and location of the oil may be appropriate in two circumstances. The first is where oil is disposed of through an exchange agreement[29] and the second is where oil is valued using NYMEX prices or ANS spot prices[30].

Exchange agreements are agreements where one person agrees to deliver oil to another person at a specified location in exchange for oil deliveries at another location.[31] In such circumstances, the value of

---

[25] 30 CFR §1206.101.
[26] 30 CFR §1206.101.
[27] 30 CFR §1206.101.
[28] 30 CFR §1206.106.
[29] 30 CFR §1206.102(d)(1)(i).
[30] 30 CFR §1206.112.
[31] 30 CFR §1206.101.

the oil exchanged may be different with respect to quality and location. Accordingly, an adjustment for these factors, defined as follows, may be appropriate:

> *Location differential* means an amount paid or received (whether in money or in barrels of oil) under an exchange agreement that results from differences in location between oil delivered in exchange and oil received in the exchange. A location differential may represent all or part of the difference between the price received for oil delivered and the price paid for oil received under a buy/sell exchange agreement.
>
> [...]
>
> *Quality differential* means an amount paid or received under an exchange agreement (whether in money or in barrels of oil) that results from differences in API gravity, sulfur content, viscosity, metals content, and other quality factors between oil delivered and oil received in the exchange. A quality differential may represent all or part of the difference between the price received for oil delivered and the price paid for oil received under a buy/sell agreement.[32]

NYMEX and ANS refer to market prices for certain grades of oil at certain market centres, and do not necessarily reflect the quality or location of the product that is actually sold from any particular lease. Accordingly, when these benchmarks are used to value oil, it may be appropriate to adjust the value for any applicable location and quality differentials.[33]

Federal Gas Royalty

Royalty payments for gas are similar to those for oil. The value of the payment is the value of production multiplied by the royalty rate in the lease.[34]

Resource, All Production, and Volume

Unlike federal oil royalties, the CFR provides valuation mechanisms for both processed gas and unprocessed gas. These mechanisms are reviewed in detail in the "value" section below.

The quality and quantity of production for which royalties are payable on unprocessed gas are determined at a "point of royalty settlement" for the lease, which is approved by the BLM for onshore leases or the BSEE for outer continental shelf leases.[35] Alternatively, if residue gas and gas plant products are being valued, quantity is based on the monthly net output of the processing plant.[36]

The lessee is required to pay a royalty for all gas produced from the lease, except gas unavoidably lost or used on, or for the benefit of, the lease, including that gas used off-lease for the benefit of the lease when

---

[32]   30 CFR §1206.101.
[33]   30 CFR §1206.103, §1206.112.
[34]   30 CFR §1202.150(a).
[35]   30 CFR §1206.154(a)(1). Under §1206.154(a)(2) a quantity/quality adjustment may be appropriate.
[36]   30 CFR §1206.154(b).

such off-lease use is permitted by the responsible authority.[37] If the loss could have been avoided, the lessee must pay royalties on the lost gas.[38] Royalties must be paid on any gas lost after the quantity basis has been determined, as is set out in 30 CFR §1206.154(d):

> (d)(1) No deductions may be made from the royalty volume or royalty value for actual or theoretical losses. Any actual loss of unprocessed gas that may be sustained prior to the royalty settlement metering or measurement point will not be subject to royalty provided that such loss is determined to have been unavoidable by BLM or BSEE, as appropriate.
>
> (2) Except as provided in paragraph (d)(1) of this section and §1202.151(c), royalties are due on 100 per cent of the volume determined in accordance with paragraphs (a) through (c) of this section. There can be no reduction in that determined volume for actual losses after the quantity basis has been determined or for theoretical losses that are claimed to have taken place. Royalties are due on 100 per cent of the value of the unprocessed gas, residue gas, and/or gas plant products as provided in this subpart, less applicable allowances. There can be no deduction from the value of the unprocessed gas, residue gas, and/or gas plant products to compensate for actual losses after the quantity basis has been determined, or for theoretical losses that are claimed to have taken place.[39]

Further, royalties may not be payable for certain other volumes of processed gas. No royalty is due for residue gas or gas plant products that are reinjected into certain reservoirs, nor is a royalty payable for certain residue gas used for the operation of a processing plant.[40]

Value

Impact of Processing

Whether the sale of a resource was at arm's length or non-arm's length is not the only relevant consideration for gas valuation. An additional consideration is whether the gas has been processed, which in this context has the following meaning:

> Processing means any process designed to remove elements or compounds (hydrocarbon and nonhydrocarbon) from gas, including absorption, adsorption, or refrigeration. Field processes which normally take place on or near the lease, such as natural pressure reduction, mechanical separation, heating, cooling, dehydration, and compression, are not considered processing. The changing of pressures and/or temperatures in a reservoir is not considered processing.[41]

---

[37]   30 CFR §1202.150(b)(1) (The responsible authority in this respect is BSEE in respect of offshore leases or BLM in respect of onshore leases).
[38]   30 CFR §1202.150(c).
[39]   30 CFR §1206.154(d).
[40]   30 CFR §1202.151.
[41]   30 CFR §1206.151.

Processing is distinct from the requirement to put the gas into marketable condition, which the lessee is required to do at no cost to the government.[42] Marketable condition for gas is defined as follows:

> *Marketable condition* means lease products which are sufficiently free from impurities and otherwise in a condition that they will be accepted by a purchaser under a sales contract typical for the field or area.[43]

Generally, putting gas into marketable condition includes gathering, compression, dehydration, and removal of acid gasses.[44]

Unprocessed Gas

The complete standards for valuing unprocessed gas, whether disposed of through an arm's length or non-arm's length contract, are set out in 30 CFR §1206.152. Generally, where gas is disposed of through an arm's length contract, its value is equal to the gross proceeds accruing to the lessee, less applicable allowances.[45] "Gross proceeds" is defined differently for gas than for oil, but this term is still dependent on the disposition of production. It should be noted that under no circumstances will the value of production for royalty purposes be less than the gross proceeds minus applicable allowances.[46] Gross proceeds is defined as follows:

> *Gross proceeds* (for royalty payment purposes) means the total monies and other consideration accruing to an oil and gas lessee for the disposition of the gas, residue gas, and gas plant products produced. Gross proceeds includes, but is not limited to, payments to the lessee for certain services such as dehydration, measurement, and/or gathering to the extent that the lessee is obligated to perform them at no cost to the Federal Government. Tax reimbursements are part of the gross proceeds accruing to a lessee even though the Federal royalty interest may be exempt from taxation. Monies and other consideration, including the forms of consideration identified in this paragraph, to which a lessee is contractually or legally entitled but which it does not seek to collect through reasonable efforts are also part of gross proceeds.[47]

Where gas is sold through a non-arm's length contract, it may be possible to use gross proceeds to determine value.[48] Alternatively, value may be determined using a "net-back" method or by considering information relevant in valuing like-quality gas. This includes gross proceeds under arm's-length contracts for like-quality gas in the same field or nearby fields or areas, posted prices for gas, prices received in arm's-

---

[42] 30 CFR §1206.152(h)(i), §1206.153(h)(i).
[43] 30 CFR §1206.151.
[44] Sarah L. Inderbitzin, "The Federal Oil and Gas Lease Marketable Condition Rule: How Far Downstream Can the Government Go?" (2007) No. 1 RMMLF-INST Paper No. 15A at II.C. Additional materials prepared by the Rocky Mountain Mineral Law Foundation are instructive on royalty payments in the American context. See Judith M. Matlock and Deborah Gibbs Tschudy, "Around the Regulations in 50 Minutes – A Practical Application of the Federal and Indian Oil & Gas Valuation Regulations" (2007) No. 1 RMMLF-INST Paper No. 2, and Peter J. Schaumberg and Geoffrey Heath, "Legal Foundation for Federal and Indian Royalty Valuation and Management" (2007) No. 1 RMMLF-INST Paper No. 1.
[45] 30 CFR §1206.152(a), §1206.152(b).
[46] 30 CFR §1206.152(h), §1206.153(h).
[47] 30 CFR §1206.151.
[48] 30 CFR §1206.153(c)(1).

length spot sales of gas, other reliable public sources of price or market information, and other information as to the particular lease operation or the saleability of the gas.[49]

Processed Gas

While royalties for unprocessed gas depend on the value of the production and the royalty rate in the lease,[50] additional factors must be considered when determining the royalty on processed gas. In particular, gas plant products and residue gas must be considered and adjusted for applicable transportation and processing allowances:

> The value of production, for royalty purposes, of gas subject to this section shall be the combined value of the residue gas and all gas plant products determined pursuant to this section, plus the value of any condensate recovered downstream of the point of royalty settlement without resorting to processing determined pursuant to §1206.102 of this part, less applicable transportation allowances and processing allowances determined pursuant to this subpart.[51]

Similar to the valuation of unprocessed gas, when valuing processed gas there are separate mechanisms which take into account whether the resource is disposed of through an arm's length or non-arm's length contract. The complete standards for valuing processed gas are set out in 30 CFR §1206.153.

Deductions and Allowances

If gas is valued using the processed gas standards, there is a deduction for processing.[52] This allows royalty to be paid on the value of the resource only, and not the added value of processing. If the unprocessed standards are used, a processing deduction is not applicable.

Where the value of processed or unprocessed gas has been determined at a point off the lease, the value of gas under the processed standards or the unprocessed standards may be deducted by a transportation allowance.[53] Standards for determining transportation allowances for gas are set out in 30 CFR §1206.157.

Annually

Royalty payments are made monthly, not annually.[54] Accordingly, the regulatory scheme in the United States provides little guidance on the meaning of "annually" in the context of Article 82.

Site

Under Article 82, there is no royalty payable for the first five years of production at a "site". For the purposes of interpreting Article 82, this period is analogous to royalty relief provisions found in the CFR.

---

[49] 30 CFR §1206.152(c).
[50] 30 CFR §1202.150(a).
[51] 30 CFR §1206.153(a)(2).
[52] 30 CFR §1206.153(a)(2).
[53] 30 CFR §1206.156.
[54] 30 CFR §1218.50.

While royalties under the CFR are payable according to the area set out in the lease, relief from royalty payments does not always depend on the lease area. Accordingly, the administration of royalty relief under the CFR is instructive for determining what "site" means in this context.

The CFR sets out numerous types of royalty relief. While it is beyond the scope of this analysis to provide a comprehensive review of royalty relief, several examples highlight the difficulty with respect to defining the scope of the "site" for which royalty suspension should apply.

Royalties may be suspended for certain volumes of production (a "royalty suspension volume") from some deep water offshore leases. Although this relief will decrease the royalty that is payable under the lease, certain royalty suspension volumes[55] are not available for individual leases, but for particular "fields", which are defined on the basis of geologic boundaries:

> *Field* means an area consisting of a single reservoir or multiple reservoirs all grouped on, or related to, the same general geological structural feature or stratigraphic trapping condition. Two or more reservoirs may be in a field, separated vertically by intervening impervious strata or laterally by local geologic barriers, or both.[56]

In certain circumstances royalty suspension volumes may be applied on a project basis,[57] or applied to production from particular wells,[58]

Under certain regulations a suspension of royalties may be available on the basis of the geographic boundaries of the lease itself, as opposed to the boundaries of the producing field.[59] Further, where a portion of a lease is unitized, royalty suspension is still applied on a lease basis and not on a unit basis:

> If a qualified ultra-deep well on your lease is within a unitized portion of your lease, the RSV ["*Royalty Suspension Volume*"] earned by that well under this section applies only to your lease and not to other leases within the unit or to the unit as a whole.[60]

All Production

In its calls for bids the federal government has indicated that for the purposes of Article 82, first production begins on the first day of commercial production excluding test production.

With respect to royalty suspension volumes, the CFR distinguishes between "production" and "test production".[61] This also suggests that the two types of production may be distinguishable for royalty purposes. This interpretation is supported by production reporting regulations, which exempt operators of certain leases from submitting certain production reports to the Office of Natural Resources Revenue in

---

[55] See 30 CFR §203.60-203.80, in particular §203.69(a).
[56] 30 CFR §203.0.
[57] 30 CFR §203.69.
[58] *e.g.* 30 CFR §203.33-34, §203.43.
[59] *e.g.* 30 CFR §560.112, 560.120-560.124 (see also *Santa Fe Snyder Corp., et al v. Norton*, 385 F(3d) 884 (5th Cir 2004)).
[60] 30 CFR §203.32(a).
[61] *e.g.* 30 CFR §203.33.

circumstances where production is limited to test production.[62] Nonetheless, test production is not explicitly discussed in the valuation regulations set out in the CFR.

Contributions in Kind

The CFR states that oil and gas royalties are to be paid in "value" unless the Office of Natural Resources Revenue requires payment in kind.[63] However, the government's royalty in kind programme ended on September 30, 2010.[64] Although the programme has been terminated, federal laws on royalties in kind continue to be informative for the purposes of determining how royalty in kind may be administered.

The United States Code contains guidance on this programme, which treats the Article 82 considerations in largely the same manner as the CFR with respect to petroleum valuation. For example, the lessee is required to put the royalty production into marketable condition at no cost to the government.[65] Further, if the lessee processes the royalty gas or delivers the royalty oil at a point not on or adjacent to the lease area, the lessee may be reimbursed for reasonable costs of processing or transportation (excluding gathering), as applicable.[66] The government may only take its royalty in kind if it would provide a benefit to the United States that is greater than or equal to the benefits that would be received for a royalty taken in value.[67] Notably, there continue to be valid regulations, contained in the CFR, on the sale of royalty oil to certain eligible refiners.[68]

---

[62]   30 CFR §1210.102.
[63]   30 CFR §1202.100(a), §1202.150(a).
[64]   "Interior Completing Close-Out of Royalty in Kind Program" (24 September 2010), online: *U.S. Department of the Interior* <https://www.doi.gov/news/pressreleases/Interior-Completing-Close-Out-of-Royalty-in-Kind-Program>.
[65]   42 USC §15902(b)(2).
[66]   42 USC §15902(c).
[67]   42 USC §15902(d).
[68]   30 CFR §1208.

BRAZIL

Resource	Royalty is payable on natural gas and crude oil, not the products that result from refining. Volume and quality of production are determined at a "production measurement point" defined in the applicable development plan.
All Production/Volume	Royalty is calculated using the "total production volume", which excludes reinjected natural gas, and reasonable quantities of natural gas flared for safety or other operational needs. Royalty is payable on other resources that are lost, flared, or used in execution of operations. Royalty is due for test production if it is used economically.
Value	Value is a product of the production volume and the reference price. Reference price is the higher of (1) the sale price at fair market value, or (2) a minimum price set by the National Agency of Petroleum. Where sale prices are used to calculate royalty, it excludes tax and transportation.
Site	Royalty is payable by field, defined in geological terms.
Payments	Payments are made in Brazilian currency. If conversion is required for a sale, the monthly average of the official daily exchange rates for the purchase of foreign currency, set by the Central Bank of Brazil, for the month in which the sale occurred is used.
Contributions in kind	-
Annually	Royalty is payable monthly. Certain additional participation payments are payable quarterly, according to the calendar quarter.

Introduction

In Brazil, the royalty regime for minerals and petroleum resources are separate. The royalty regime for minerals does not form part of this review. Lei Ordinária 9.478, de 6.8.97 ("Law 9.478/97")[69] states that the federal government owns the exploration and production rights of oil, natural gas and other fluid hydrocarbons in Brazil, including onshore lands, territorial waters, the continental shelf, and the exclusive economic zone, and that the National Agency of Petroleum (the "ANP") is responsible for the administration of resources in these areas.[70] Also under Law 9.478/97, concessionaires are required to make royalty payments and may be required to make payments to the Brazilian Government for "special participation" in respect of petroleum production.[71]

---

[69] Lei Ordinária 9.478, de 6.8.97 ("L. 9.478/97"), online: *Brazil* < http://www.planalto.gov.br/ccivil_03/Leis/L9478.htm> (Portuguese), *EI SourceBook* < http://www.eisourcebook.org/cms/Brazil,%20Exploration%20and%20Production%20of%20Oil%20&%20Gas%20Legislation.pdf> (English).

[70] L. 9.478/97, art. 21.

[71] L. 9.478/97, art. 45.

Royalty

Resource

Royalty payments depend on the produced volume and quality of crude oil and natural gas. These terms are defined separately from "oil by-products", suggesting that royalty should be paid on the resource in its natural state:

> I – Oil: any and all liquid hydrocarbon in its natural state, such as crude oil and condensate;
>
> II – Natural Gas: any hydrocarbon that remains in gaseous state under normal atmospheric conditions, produced directly from oil or gas reservoirs, including wet, dry and residual gases, and rare gases;
>
> III – Oil by-products: products derived from oil refining;[72]

Royalty is payable from the start up date of commercial production for each field.[73] Volume and quality of production of resources are determined at a "production measurement point",[74] which is defined as follows:

> IV - Production Measurement Points: points to be mandatorily defined in the Development Plan of each field, proposed by the concessionaire and approved by the ANP, in the terms of the Concession Agreement, where the volumetric measurement of the crude oil or natural gas produced in such field will be carried on, expressed in metric units of volume adopted by the ANP and using the standard condition of measurement, and where the concessionaire shall assume the ownership of the respective supervised production volumes, and being subject to the payment of applicable taxes and the respective legal and contractual participation;[75]

All Production and Volume

Article 47 of Law 9.478/97 states that the calculation criteria for royalty payments will be set out by presidential decree.[76] Decreto 2.705, de 3.8.98 ("Decree 2.705/98") provides these criteria. In particular, Article 12 indicates that the royalty for a field is calculated as a percentage of the "total production volume" multiplied by the "reference price" for the resource:

> Article 12. The value of the royalties to be paid monthly in relation to a field, shall be determined by multiplying the equivalent to ten per cent of the total production volume of crude oil and

---

[72] L. 9.478/97, art. 6.
[73] L. 9.478/97, art. 47.
[74] Decreto 2.705, de 3.8.98 ("D. 2.705/98"), art. 4, online: *Brazil* <http://www.planalto.gov.br/ccivil_03/decreto/D2705.htm> (Portuguese), *ANP* < http://www.anp.gov.br/brasil-rounds/round1/docs/ldoc02_en.pdf> (English).
[75] D. 2.705/98, art. 3.
[76] L. 9.478/97, art. 47, para. 2.

natural gas of the field during such month, by its respective reference prices, established in Chapter IV of this Decree. [...] [77]

By definition, "total production volume" includes resources that are lost, flared, or used in the execution of operations. However, reinjected natural gas, and reasonable quantities of natural gas flared for safety or other operational needs do not form part of production:

> XI - Total Production Volume: sum of all and any amounts of crude oil and natural gas extracted from each field monthly, expressed in the metric volume units adopted by the ANP, including the amounts of crude oil and natural gas lost under the concessionaire's responsibility; the amounts of crude oil and natural gas used in the execution of operations in the same field and the amounts of natural gas burned through flares instead of through commercial operations, and excluding only the amounts of natural gas reinjected in the reserve and the amounts of natural gas burned through flares, for safety reasons or for a proven operational need, as long as this burn is of a reasonable quantity, compatible with the usual practices of the oil industry, and being previously approved by the ANP or later justified by a written notice to the ANP within 48 hours from its occurrence.[78]

Until 2014 it was unclear how test production should be treated for royalty purposes. On August 13, 2014, the ANP released Resolution 862/2014 stating that royalties are payable on test production from the exploration phase if there is an economic use of the extracted hydrocarbons.[79]

Value

The value of the royalty to be paid monthly is the total production volume of a field multiplied by its respective reference price,[80] which is defined as follows:

> V - Reference Price: price by unit of volume, expressed in Brazilian currency, for the crude oil, natural gas or condensate produced in each field, to be determined by the ANP, according to the provisions of Articles 8 and 9 of this Decree;[81]

There are two ways to set the reference price used to calculate royalties. Concessionaires will use the higher of the sale price (at fair market price) and a minimum price established by the ANP. Reference prices do not include sales taxes, and are deemed to be shipped free on board (i.e. shipping costs are borne by the buyer). The ANP sets the minimum price as the monthly average value of similar crudes on the international market:

---

[77] D. 2.705/98, art. 12.

[78] D. 2.705/98, art. 3. See also L. 9.478/97, art. 47, para. 3, which specifies that flared gas and other losses should be considered as part of the total production volume on which royalties are payable.

[79] RD. nº 862/2014 (13 August 2014), online: *ANP* < http://rd.anp.gov.br/NXT/gateway.dll/atas/2014/reuni%C3%A3o%20n%C2%BA%20766%C2%AA%20-%2013.08.2014/ata%2Br766%2B2014.xml?fn=document-frame.htm$f=templates$3.0>.

[80] D. 2.705/98, art. 12.

[81] D. 2.705/98, art. 3.

Article 7. The reference price to be applied monthly to the produced crude oil in each field during the corresponding month, expressed in R$ (Reais) per cubic meter, at the Standard Measurement Condition, shall be equal to the crude oil weighted average of the concessionaire's sale prices, at a fair market price, or at its minimum price established by the ANP, whichever is greater.

> Paragraph 1. The sale prices mentioned in this Article shall be free of taxes applied on sales, and in the case of crude oil shipped, shall be free on board.

> [...]

> Paragraph 5. The minimum price of the crude oil extracted in each field shall be set by the ANP according to a monthly average value of the standard aggregate of up to four types of similar crude oils quoted on the international market, according to this Article.[...][82]

The references prices for natural gas sales are set using a similar method, and exclude taxes and transportation tariffs.[83]

Site

Under Decree 2.705/98, royalties are payable with respect to extraction from a "field".[84] The term "field" is not defined in Decree 2.705/98, although it is defined in geological terms with reference to reservoirs in Law 9.478/97:

> X – Reservoir: geological configuration with specific properties, bearing oil or gas, associated or not.

> [...]

> XIV – Oil or Natural Gas Field: area where oil or natural gas is produced, starting from a continuous reservoir or more than one reservoir, at variable depths, comprising production installations and equipment;[85]

However, a licence to produce is not defined by field, but by the area set out in a particular concession agreement.[86] Where a field extends for two or more concession areas, the unitization agreement will define the producers' royalty payments:

> Article 13. In case of fields extending for two or more concession areas, where different concessionaires operate, the agreement executed among the concessionaires for the unitization

---

[82] D. 2.705/98, art. 7.
[83] D. 2.705/98, art. 8.
[84] D. 2.705/98, art. 3, VII and VIII, and art. 11.
[85] L. 9.478/97, art. 6.
[86] L. 9.478/97, art. 23.

of the production, as established in Article 27 of Law No. 9,478, of 1997, shall define each concessionaire's share in the payment of royalties.[87]

Payment

Royalties are payable in Brazilian currency by the last day of the month following the month of the calculation:

> Article 18. The value of the royalties shall be calculated monthly by each concessionaire, related to each field, from the month in which occurs the Start-up Production Date of the field, and shall be paid in Brazilian currency by the last business day of the month following the month of its calculation, provided that the concessionaire shall send to the ANP a demonstrative report of the calculations, in a standard form provided by the ANP, with documents certifying the payment, before the fifth business day after the payment.

If a currency conversion for a particular sale is required, it should be performed using the monthly average of the official daily exchange rates for the purchase of foreign currency, set by the Central Bank of Brazil, for the month in which the sale occurred.[88]

Special Participation

"Special participation" applies in circumstances where there are large production volumes or high profitability, and is payable on gross production revenue less the value of royalties paid by the producer, production investments, operational costs, depreciation, and taxes.[89] "Special participation" is due quarterly during the calendar year,[90] and its calculation depends not only on the deductions set out in Law 9.478/97, but also on the location of the reservoir, the depth of production, how long the field has been in production, and the inspected quarterly production volume.[91]

---

[87] D. 2.705/98, art. 13.
[88] D. 2.705/98, art. 7, paras. 4, 10; D. 2.705/98, art. 8, para. 3
[89] L. 9.478/97, art. 50; see also D. 2.705/98, arts. 3(VII) and 22 for "special participation".
[90] D. 2.705/98, art. 25.
[91] D. 2.705/98, art. 22.

CANADA (ALBERTA)

Resource	Royalty is paid on crude oil. Quantity of royalty is calculated at the place where the oil is first measured after it is recovered.
	Royalty standards are available for the valuation of processed gas. The royalty share of natural gas is determined at a "royalty calculation point". If the gas is unprocessed, this is generally tied to the point of delivery from the gathering system, or if processed gas is being considered, at the processing or reprocessing plant.
All Production/Volume	If there are any actions that will artificially reduce the royalty share owing to the Crown, the royalty will be calculated as if that action had not taken place. Generally, flared solution gas is exempt from royalty payments. Further, royalty is not payable on certain natural gas or residue gas consumed as a fuel in operations for gathering or processing natural gas. Royalty credits for reinjected gas may be available.
Value/Contributions in kind	Regulations set out complex calculations for determining "royalty share", which is payable in kind unless otherwise indicated. The royalty rate is based on the price and quantity of the resource, and depending on the resource may be influenced by density (oil), depth of the well event, acid gas content (gas), geographic location of the well, or the length of time the well has been producing. Deductions may be allowed for the use of certain innovative technologies used to improve recovery.
	Oil royalty is generally taken in kind and delivered to the Crown at the place where it is first measured after it is recovered. Gas royalty is generally taken in value instead of in kind. The reference price used to determine value may be deducted by transportation, gathering, and processing costs.
Site	The relevant site for payment is the "well event". Alternatively, if there is a unit agreement, the "unit" may be the relevant site.
Payments	Regulations provide a mechanism to convert "royalty share" to a monetary payment, where appropriate. No currency conversion mechanism provided.
Annually	-

Introduction

Canada has a federal system of governance. Accordingly, the administration of resource development depends both on provincial and federal legislation. For the purposes of royalty payments for petroleum produced in Alberta, provincial legislation is determinative. The Provincial Crown owns approximately 80 per cent of the subsurface mineral rights in the Province.[92] Under Alberta's Mines and Minerals Act, RSA 2000, c M-17 (the "Mines and Minerals Act"),[93] the Provincial Crown has the right to receive a royalty on minerals recovered under a Crown agreement.[94]

The amount of Crown royalty on crude oil is established in the Petroleum Royalty Regulation, 2009, Alta Reg 222/2008 (the "Petroleum Royalty Regulation")[95] while the royalty on gas is established in the Natural Gas Royalty Regulation, 2009, Alta Reg 221/2008 (the "Natural Gas Royalty Regulation").[96] Royalty structures for other resources, such as oil sands, do not form part of this review.

The Alberta regime is set to change in the near future. The new system for oil and gas royalties will likely be based on a "revenue minus costs" structure, which will allow producers to pay a reduced royalty until certain capital costs have been recouped.[97]

Oil Royalty

Resource and Contribution in Kind

Under the Petroleum Royalty Regulation, royalty is payable on crude oil and solution gas,[98] which are defined as follows:

> 1(1) In this Regulation,
>
> [...]
>
> (b) "crude oil" means a mixture mainly of pentanes and heavier hydrocarbons
>
> > (i)   that may be contaminated with sulphur compounds,
> >
> > (ii)   that is recovered or is recoverable at a well from an underground reservoir, and
> >
> > (iii)   that is liquid at the conditions under which its volume is measured or estimated,
>
> and includes all other hydrocarbon mixtures so recovered or recoverable except natural gas, field condensate or crude bitumen;
>
> [...]
>
> (m) "solution gas" means
>
> > (i)   gas that is separated from crude oil after recovery from a well, and

---

92   "Tenure" *Alberta Energy*, online: *Alberta* <http://www.energy.gov.ab.ca/OurBusiness/tenure.asp>.

93   Mines and Minerals Act, RSA 2000 c M-17 ("Mines and Minerals Act").

94   Mines and Minerals Act, s. 33.

95   Petroleum Royalty Regulation, 2009, Alta Reg 222/2008 ("Petroleum Royalty Regulation").

96   Natural Gas Royalty Regulation, 2009, Alta Reg 221/2008("Natural Gas Royalty Regulation").

97   "Alberta at a Crossroads: Royalty Review Advisory Panel Report" (January 2015), online: Alberta Government <http://www.energy.alberta.ca/Org/pdfs/RoyaltyReportJan2016.pdf>.

98   Petroleum Royalty Regulation, s. 6.

> (ii)   gas that is dissolved in crude oil under initial reservoir conditions and includes any of that gas that evolves as a result of changes in pressure or temperature, or both, due to human disturbance; [...][99]

A distinguishing feature of the Alberta oil royalty scheme is that the royalty is generally deliverable in kind, unless otherwise provided by the regulations. Under the Mines and Minerals Act, the quantity of the resource that comprises the royalty is calculated and delivered to the Crown at the place where the mineral is first measured after it is recovered:

> 34 (3)   Except as otherwise provided by the regulations,
>
> (a)   the royalty reserved to the Crown in right of Alberta shall be deliverable in kind,
>
> (b)   the quantity of the royalty reserved to the Crown in right of Alberta shall be calculated at the place where the mineral is first measured after it is recovered, and
>
> (c)   the royalty reserved to the Crown in right of Alberta shall be delivered to the Crown at the place at which the quantity of the royalty is calculated.[100]

Royalty Share of Production

Under the Petroleum Royalty Regulation the royalty for oil is calculated as a volume, not as a value, as royalty is generally demanded in kind:

$$\text{royalty in cubic metres} = \text{quantity} \times (r_p\% + r_q\%) \times \text{Crown interest}[101]$$

All Production and Volume

For this calculation, "quantity" is the volume of production on which royalty is deliverable, and is defined as "[...] the monthly production in cubic metres of crude oil from a well event according to the records of the Regulator".[102] If there are any actions that will artificially reduce the royalty share owing to the Crown, whether for oil or gas, the royalty will be calculated as if that action had not taken place, as is stated in the Mines and Minerals Act:

> 37   If, in the opinion of the Minister, the result of one or more acts, agreements, arrangements, transactions or operations is to artificially or unduly reduce
>
> (a)   the Crown's royalty share in respect of a mineral,
>
> (b)   the amount owing on account of a money royalty,
>
> (c)   the amount owing in respect of the disposal of the Crown's royalty share   by an agent, or
>
> (d)   the amount owing on account of royalty compensation,

---

[99]   Petroleum Royalty Regulation, s. 1(1).
[100]   Mines and Minerals Act, s. 34(3).
[101]   Petroleum Royalty Regulation, sch., s. 2(1).
[102]   Petroleum Royalty Regulation, sch., s. 1(c).

the royalty share or the amount owing shall be calculated as if the act, agreement, arrangement, transaction or operation had not taken place.[103]

Royalty Rate

The terms r_p% and r_q% are the price and quantity components of the royalty rate, which ordinarily ranges from a minimum of zero per cent to a maximum of either 40 or 50 per cent.[104] The royalty rate is dependent on the production volume, the price of the product, and the type of oil produced. The categories of oil that will receive their own "par price", which is used to calculate the appropriate royalty rate, range from light to ultra heavy.[105]

Crown Interest

By including a term for "Crown interest" the royalty equation accounts for the fact that the Crown may not be the owner of all mineral resources extracted, and that the royalty is payable to the Crown for the Crown's share only.

Deductions and Adjustments

The royalty may be adjusted to account for the costs of certain innovative technologies used to improve petroleum resource recovery.[106]

Natural Gas Royalty

There are two primary steps in determining the royalty payment for gas. The first is to determine the Crown's royalty share of the resource and the second is to value that royalty share, since gas royalties are not generally taken in kind.

Resource and Contribution in Kind

Both processed and unprocessed gas may be valued under the Natural Gas Royalty Regulation. The place at which the Crown's royalty share of natural gas, gas products or field condensate is to be calculated is called the "royalty calculation point", and is determined based on the type of product being valued. If the gas is unprocessed, the royalty calculation is generally tied to the point of delivery from the gathering system. If the gas is processed, the royalty calculation point is generally set at the processing or reprocessing plant:

---

[103] Mines and Minerals Act, s. 37.
[104] Petroleum Royalty Regulation, sch., s. 2(2); however, under the Petroleum Royalty Regulation, s. 6.1 the royalty can be capped at 5%.
[105] Petroleum Royalty Regulation, s. 5.
[106] Petroleum Royalty Regulation, s. 7; "Innovative Energy Technologies Program" *Alberta Energy*, online: *Alberta* <http://www.energy.alberta.ca/NaturalGas/729.asp>.

9 Unless the Minister otherwise determines in a particular case, the place at which the Crown's royalty share of natural gas, gas products or field condensate is to be calculated is the place determined in accordance with the following rules:

- (a) the Crown's royalty share of natural gas referred to in section 8(1) must be calculated at

  - (i) the last point of measurement before the natural gas is delivered from the gathering system in which it is transported, or

  - (i) the point of delivery under the disposition, if the natural gas is disposed of and the point of delivery is upstream from the point referred to in subclause (i);

- (b) the Crown's royalty share of pentanes plus referred to in section 8(2) must be calculated at the first point of measurement after the pentanes plus are delivered from the gathering system;

- (c) the Crown's royalty share of residue gas and other gas products referred to in section 8(4)(a) must be calculated at the plant gate of the gas processing plant at which the residue gas and other gas products are obtained;

- (d) the Crown's royalty share of residue gas referred to in section 8(4)(b)(i) must be calculated at the plant gate of the last of the reprocessing plants referred to in that subclause;

- (e) the Crown's royalty share of a gas product referred to in section 8(4)(b)(ii) must be calculated at the plant gate of the reprocessing plant at which the gas product is obtained;

- (f) the Crown's royalty share of field condensate must be calculated at its first point of measurement after being obtained from natural gas or solution gas.[107]

The Crown's royalty share transfers to the owner of the lessee's share of the gas immediately downstream of the royalty calculation point. Where this title transfer takes place, royalty compensation must be paid to the Crown in value instead of being delivered in volume:

15(1) The Crown's title to the Crown's royalty share of natural gas and gas products is automatically transferred

- (a) at the point immediately downstream from the royalty calculation point for the natural gas or gas products, or

- (b) in the case of sulphur,

  - (i) at the place where it is solidified at the site of the gas processing plant or reprocessing plant at which it is obtained, or

  - (ii) at the place where it leaves the gas processing plant or reprocessing plant at which it is obtained, where it leaves the plant in liquid form without having first been solidified,

---

[107] Natural Gas Royalty Regulation, s. 9.

to the person who is, in relation to that royalty share, the owner of the lessee's share of the natural gas or gas products.

(2) When the Crown's title to the Crown's royalty share of natural gas or a gas product is transferred pursuant to subsection (1), royalty compensation is payable to the Crown in accordance with this Regulation in respect of that royalty share.[...][108]

Royalty Share of Production

The mechanism used to determine the royalty share of the resource will depend on the gas in question, the degree to which it is has been processed, and how or where it will be disposed, consumed, or delivered.[109] In general, determining the royalty quantity of gas is similar to the determination for oil. The Crown's royalty share of production is a product of the quantities of gases produced or processed and the appropriate royalty rates.[110]

All Production and Volume

Generally, flared solution gas is exempt from royalty payments.[111] Further, royalty is not payable on certain natural gas or residue gas consumed as a fuel in operations for gathering or processing natural gas:

13(1) No royalty is payable to the Crown,

(a) on natural gas or residue gas consumed as a fuel in operations for gathering or processing natural gas recovered pursuant to a Crown lease, or on residue gas consumed as a fuel in operations for reprocessing residue gas obtained from natural gas recovered pursuant to a Crown lease, where

(i) the natural gas so consumed is recovered from the same pool as the natural gas that is gathered or processed, or

(ii) the residue gas so consumed is obtained from natural gas recovered from the same pool as the natural gas that is gathered or processed,

as the case may be, including consumption as a fuel for the purpose of generating electricity and steam in a power plant that is provided for such operations in exchange for the fuel;

(b) with approval of the Minister given before January 1, 1994, on natural gas, residue gas or solution gas consumed as a fuel in operations for the recovery or processing of oil sands or oil sands products conducted under a commercial oil sands scheme under the *Oil Sands Conservation Act*, where the scheme is also the subject of a contract entered into pursuant to section 9(a) of the Act;

(c) unless the Minister directs otherwise in any case, on solution gas consumed as a fuel in operations for the recovery or processing of oil sands or oil sands products

---

[108] Natural Gas Royalty Regulation, s. 15.
[109] Natural Gas Royalty Regulation, s. 8.
[110] Natural Gas Royalty Regulation, sch. 1, s. 2, sch. 2.
[111] Natural Gas Royalty Regulation, s. 14.

that is subject to royalty under the *Oil Sands Royalty Regulation, 2009*, where the consumed solution gas and the oil sands or oil sands products recovered or processed in such operations are recovered pursuant to the same agreement;

(d) unless the Minister directs otherwise in any case, on any natural gas, residue gas or solution gas other than natural gas, residue gas or solution gas referred to in clause (b) or (c), consumed as fuel for drilling or production operations in respect of a well drilled pursuant to an agreement.[...][112]

Notably, if there are any actions that will artificially reduce the royalty share owing to the Crown, whether for oil or gas, the royalty will be calculated as if that action had not taken place.[113] Further, royalty credits may be available for certain reinjected gas.[114]

Royalty Rate and Adjustments

The royalty rate is unique for each well event, and is generally a function of price and quantity, which will depend on the complexities of the individual well in question. In particular, the royalty rate may be influenced by the depth of the well event[115] and the acid gas content of the resource.[116]

Further, adjustments for certain geographic locations[117] and the length of time for which the well event has been in production[118] may be appropriate.

Value, Including Deductions and Adjustments

Once the royalty share of production has been determined, it is necessary to calculate the value of the royalty payment. The royalty share of production is a volume, but under the regulations the liability for royalty compensation may be required in value.

The royalty payment is calculated as the product of the "net gas reference price" and the royalty share, less the cost of conservation gas and costs incurred for the use of certain innovative technologies that improve resource recovery.[119] The "net gas reference price"[120] is equal to the "aggregate gas reference price",[121] set out under the regulation, minus a transportation allowance.[122]

Once the royalty payment is determined, further deductions may be appropriate. In particular, costs incurred in gathering, processing, reprocessing, or handling the Crown's royalty share must be deducted from the royalty compensation that is otherwise payable:

---

[112] Natural Gas Royalty Regulation, s. 13(1).
[113] Mines and Minerals Act, s. 37.
[114] Natural Gas Royalty Regulation, s. 17.
[115] Natural Gas Royalty Regulation, sch. 2, s. 6.
[116] Natural Gas Royalty Regulation, sch. 2, s. 5.
[117] Natural Gas Royalty Regulation, ss. 7(10)(a), 7(10)(c), and sch. 1, s. 2.
[118] Natural Gas Royalty Regulation, sch. 1, s. 3.
[119] Natural Gas Royalty Regulation, sch. 1, s. 7.
[120] Natural Gas Royalty Regulation, sch. 1, s. 6.
[121] Natural Gas Royalty Regulation, sch. 1, s. 4.
[122] Natural Gas Royalty Regulation, sch.1, s. 5.

18   (1)   In this section, "facility" does not include a gas injection facility or commercial storage facility.

       (2)   The costs and allowances to which the Minister consents and that are incurred

       (a)   in gathering or processing the Crown's royalty share of natural gas or reprocessing the Crown's royalty share of residue gas, and

       (b)   in handling the Crown's royalty share of gas products within a gas processing plant or reprocessing plant after the place in the plant where the Crown's royalty share is calculated

must, subject to this section, be deducted from the royalty compensation otherwise payable.[...][123]

Site

The relevant site for royalty calculation is generally the "well event",[124] which is defined in the Petroleum Royalty Regulation as follows:

       1(1)   [...]

       (o)   well event" means

                (i)   a part of a well completed in a zone and given a unique well identifier by the Regulator,

                (ii)   parts of a well completed in 2 or more zones and given a single unique well identifier by the Regulator,

                (iii)   a part of a well completed in and recovering crude oil from a zone but which has not yet been given a unique well identifier by the Regulator, or

                (iv)   parts of a well completed in and recovering crude oil from 2 or more zones during the period when the parts are considered by the Minister as a single well event for the purposes of this Regulation and before the Regulator makes a decision whether or not to give the parts a single unique well identifier;[125]

If there is a unitization agreement, the "unit" may be the relevant location for calculating the appropriate royalty.[126]

The Alberta Government provides various categories of royalty relief. The geographic basis on which this relief is available is informative for determining the meaning of "site" in Article 82. Relief in the form of a capped royalty rate may be available for new production on a "well event" basis, as is provided in the New Well Royalty Regulation, Alta Reg 32/2011.[127] In this context, the "well event" is the relevant "site".

---

[123]   Natural Gas Royalty Regulation, s. 18.
[124]   Petroleum Royalty Regulation, sch., ss. 1(c), 2(1). See also the Natural Gas Royalty Regulation, s. 8.
[125]   Petroleum Royalty Regulation, s. 1(1).
[126]   Natural Gas Royalty Regulation, s. 11; Petroleum Royalty Regulation s. 8.
[127]   New Well Royalty Regulation, Alta Reg 32/2011.

AUSTRALIA

Resource	Determined at wellhead.
All Production/Volume	Wellhead production minus certain petroleum that is unavoidably lost before the quantity of petroleum is measured, used for the purposes of operations related to exploration or recovery, flared or vented in connection with petroleum recovery operations, or returned to a natural reservoir.
Value	-
Contributions in kind	-
Site	Site for royalty payment is established by the permit area, lease area, or licence area. Relief is available for certain uneconomic wells.
Payments	-
Annually	Royalty is payable monthly.

Introduction

Australia has a federal system of governance. Accordingly, the administration of resource development depends both on state and commonwealth legislation. Significant offshore hydrocarbon reserves are located on the North West Shelf which is located off the coast of Western Australia. The Australian Commonwealth Government has developed a royalty regime under the Offshore Petroleum (Royalty) Act 2006 (Cth) (the "Royalty Act"),[128] which applies to a small number of North West Shelf titles. The Royalty Act, reviewed below, is instructive for the interpretation of Article 82.

It should be noted that although individual states have developed resource royalty laws, these various laws do not form part of this review. Further, royalty is only one aspect of resource revenue administration in Australia. The broader Australian taxation system that impacts resource developers is not reviewed in this report.

Petroleum exploration and development in "offshore areas" is governed by the Offshore Petroleum and Greenhouse Gas Storage Act 2006 (Cth) (the "OPGGSA")[129] which applies for the purposes of interpreting terms used in the Royalty Act.[130] In general, an "offshore area" starts three nautical miles from the baseline from which the breadth of the territorial sea is measured and extends seaward to the outer limits of the continental shelf.[131] However, the royalty set out in the Royalty Act does not apply to all offshore areas; it

---

[128] Offshore Petroleum (Royalty) Act 2006 (Cth) ("Royalty Act").
[129] Offshore Petroleum and Greenhouse Gas Storage Act 2006 (Cth) ("OPGGSA"), s. 4.
[130] Royalty Act, s. 3.
[131] OPGGSA, s. 4.

applies in respect of exploration permits, retention leases, or production licences for the North West Shelf only.[132]

Resource

Royalty is payable on "petroleum", which is defined to include naturally occurring hydrocarbons, whether in a gaseous, liquid, or solid state.[133] The value and quantity of the resource on which a royalty is payable are determined at the wellhead,[134] suggesting that it is not the processed resource which is valued. The meaning of "wellhead" is defined as follows in the Royalty Act:

11 Meaning of *wellhead*

For the purposes of this Act, the *wellhead*, in relation to any petroleum, is:

(a)   such valve station as is agreed between:

        (i)   the registered holder of the petroleum exploration permit, petroleum retention lease or petroleum production licence; and

        (ii)   the State Minister; or

(b)   if there is no agreement within such period as the State Minister allows - such valve station as the State Minister determines to be that wellhead.[135]

All Production and Quantity

Quantity is determined using a measuring device installed at the wellhead:

13 Quantity of petroleum recovered

For the purposes of this Act, the quantity of petroleum recovered by the registered holder of a petroleum exploration permit, petroleum retention lease or petroleum production licence from a well during a period is taken to be:

(a)   the quantity measured during that period by a measuring device:

        (i)   approved by the State Minister; and

        (ii)   installed at the wellhead or at such other place as the State Minister approves; or

(b)   if:

        (i)   no such measuring device is so installed; or

        (ii)   the State Minister or the Joint Authority is not satisfied that the quantity of petroleum recovered by the registered holder from that well has been properly or accurately measured by such a measuring device;

---

[132]   Royalty Act, s. 5.
[133]   Royalty Act, s. 5, OPGGSA, s. 7 ("petroleum").
[134]   Royalty Act, ss. 12-13.
[135]   Royalty Act, s. 11.

the quantity determined by the State Minister as being the quantity recovered by the registered holder from that well during that period.[136]

The legislation sets out certain volumes on which royalty is not payable. In particular, royalty is not payable on petroleum that is unavoidably lost before the quantity of petroleum is measured, used for the purposes of operations related to exploration or recovery, flared or vented in connection with petroleum recovery operations, or returned to a natural reservoir:

10   Exemptions from royalty

(1)   Royalty under this Act:

(a)   is not payable in relation to petroleum that the State Minister is satisfied was unavoidably lost before the quantity of that petroleum was ascertained; and

(b)   is not payable in relation to petroleum if:

(i)   the State Minister is satisfied that the petroleum was used by the registered holder of the petroleum exploration permit, petroleum retention lease or petroleum production licence for the purposes of petroleum exploration operations or operations for the recovery of petroleum; and

(ii)   the use did not contravene the *Offshore Petroleum and Greenhouse Gas Storage Act 2006* or regulations under that Act; and

(c)   is not payable in relation to petroleum if:

(i)   the State Minister is satisfied that the petroleum has been flared or vented in connection with operations for the recovery of petroleum; and

(ii)   the flaring or venting did not contravene the *Offshore Petroleum and Greenhouse Gas Storage Act 2006* or regulations under that Act.

(2)   If petroleum has been recovered by the registered holder of:

(a)   a petroleum exploration permit; or

(b)   a petroleum retention lease; or

(c)   a petroleum production licence;

royalty under this Act is not payable in relation to the petroleum because of that recovery if:

(d)   the State Minister is satisfied that the petroleum has been returned to a natural reservoir; and

(e)   the return of the petroleum to the reservoir did not contravene the *Offshore Petroleum and Greenhouse Gas Storage Act 2006* or regulations under that Act.

(3)   Subsection (2) does not affect the liability of that or any other registered holder to pay royalty in relation to petroleum that is recovered from that natural reservoir.[137]

---

[136]   Royalty Act, s. 13.

Value

Under the Royalty Act, royalty is payable on the wellhead value of petroleum.[138] However, the Royalty Act is of limited use for determining how the Article 82 term "value" should be interpreted since it does not provide a valuation mechanism. Instead, the Royalty Act states that the value of petroleum at the wellhead is the value agreed upon between the proponent and the state government, or alternatively, by the state government alone:

> 12   Meaning of *value*
>
> For the purposes of this Act, the *value* at the wellhead of any petroleum is:
>
> (a)   such amount as is agreed between:
>
> (i)   the registered holder of the petroleum exploration permit, petroleum retention lease or petroleum production licence; and
>
> (ii)   the State Minister; or
>
> (b)   if there is no agreement within such period as the State Minister allows - such amount as the State Minister determines to be that value.[139]

Site

Royalty is payable on all petroleum recovered by the registered holder in the permit area, lease area, or licence area,[140] which are constituted by the block or blocks that are the subject of the permit, lease, or licence.[141] Blocks are not defined with respect to the geological attributes of the site. Instead, the offshore is divided into blocks based on set units of latitude and longitude.[142] Nonetheless, royalty relief in respect of reduced recovery is determined on a well basis,[143] not on the basis of the relevant permit, lease, or licence area.

Royalty is payable on all petroleum recovered by the holder of a permit, lease, or licence in a "royalty period" beginning at or after the commencement date of s. 5 of the Royalty Act.[144] Since s. 5 commenced on July 1, 2008,[145] the statutory definition of "royalty period" is instructive in determining when royalty obligations arise. Using the definition set out in s. 4 of the Royalty Act, the monthly payment obligation arises when the relevant permit, lease, or licence comes into force:

---

[137]   Royalty Act, s. 10.
[138]   Royalty Act, s. 6.
[139]   Royalty Act, s. 12.
[140]   Royalty Act, s. 5.
[141]   OPGGSA, s. 7 ("lease area", "licence area", and "permit area").
[142]   OPGGSA, ss. 7 ("block"), 33, 282.
[143]   Royalty Act, s. 9.
[144]   Royalty Act, s. 5.
[145]   Royalty Act, s. 2.

4 Definitions

In this Act:

[...]

royalty period, in relation to a North West Shelf exploration permit, a North West Shelf retention lease or a North West Shelf production licence, means:

(a)   the period beginning on:

(i)   the day on which the permit, lease or licence comes or came into force; and

(ii)   ending at the end of the month in which that day occurs; and

(b)   each later month. [...][146]

The royalty in relation to petroleum recovered during a royalty period is due and payable at the end of the next royalty period.[147]

---

[146]   Royalty Act, s. 4.
[147]   OPGGSA, s. 631.

NIGERIA

Resource	Royalty is charged on crude oil, casing-head petroleum spirit, and natural gas. Crude oil ("crude") means oil in its natural state before it has been refined or treated (excluding water and other foreign substances). Casing-head petroleum spirit ("spirit") means liquid hydrocarbons which have been obtained from natural gas by natural separation or by any chemical or physical process, and have not been refined or otherwise treated.
All Production/ Volume	The quantity of crude or spirit on which royalty is charged is the produced quantity less the following volumes: (1) crude or spirit used for the purpose of carrying out drilling and production operations, or pumping to storage and refineries; (2) crude or spirit that is injected or returned by the licensee or lessee into a formation in the relevant quarter; and (3) any reasonable pipeline or evaporating losses.
	Royalty may also be payable on natural gas sold by a licensee or lessee, not including certain flare or waste gas appropriated by the government for its own use or for any purpose approved by it.
Value	Value of crude and spirit for the purposes of royalty is a product of the reduced quantity and the appropriate price, subject to certain financial deductions. The export price of crude and spirit is established by the Minister of Petroleum Resources as the price free on board at a Nigerian port of export for crude or spirit of the gravity and quality in question. If the crude or spirit is delivered to a Nigerian refinery, the price is approved by the Director of Petroleum Resources. The price should bear a reasonable relationship to established posted prices or to prices at international trading export centres, and should have due regard for freight differentials and "other relevant factors".
	Deductions are permitted for the cost incurred in handling, treating, and storing the "reduced quantity" and in transporting the quantity of crude and spirit from the field to a tankship at a Nigerian port or to a refinery in Nigeria.
	The royalty on crude and spirit is a percentage of the resource value. The rate depends on the production volume and the depth of the water in which production takes place.
Site	Royalties are payable for resources produced from each field operated by the licensee or lessee in the "relevant area", which is defined as the area affected by the licence or lease.
Payments	-
Contributions in kind	-
Annually	Royalty payments are due one month after the end of the quarter and a quarter is defined as a calendar quarter.

Introduction

One of the primary statutes under which royalty is charged in Nigeria is the Petroleum Act 1969 (the "Petroleum Act"). The Petroleum Act applies to all land and land covered by water that is in Nigeria, under the territorial waters of Nigeria, forms part of the continental shelf, or forms part of the Exclusive Economic Zone of Nigeria.[148] Under the Petroleum Act, the continental shelf is defined as follows:

> "continental shelf" means the seabed and subsoil of those submarine areas adjacent to the coast of Nigeria the surface of which lies at a depth no greater than 200 metres (or, where its natural resources are capable of exploitation, at any depth) below the surface of the sea, excluding so much of those areas as lies below the territorial waters of Nigeria;[149]

The Petroleum (Production and Drilling) Regulations 1969 (the "Regulations") are made pursuant to s. 9 of the Petroleum Act. The Regulations set out a major component of Nigeria's royalty scheme and are reviewed below. It should be noted that the royalty set out in the Petroleum Act and the Regulations is only one aspect of resource revenue administration in Nigeria. Other statutes, as well as special terms and conditions attached to leases and licences[150] may also impact royalty payments and the taxation of petroleum activities.

Resource

The resources on which the Nigerian Government charges royalty include crude oil and casing-head petroleum spirit,[151] which are by definition unrefined. Crude oil ("crude") is defined in the Petroleum Act as "...oil in its natural state before it has been refined or treated (excluding water and other foreign substances)".[152] Natural gas liquids extracted from natural gas and spiked into the oil stream are treated as oil for royalty purposes.[153] Casing-head petroleum spirit ("spirit") is defined in the Regulations as follows:

> "casing-head petroleum spirit" means any liquid hydrocarbons which—
>
> (a)   have been obtained from natural gas by natural separation or by any chemical or physical process; and
>
> (b)   have not been refined or otherwise treated;[154]

Royalty may also be payable on natural gas that is extracted and sold.[155] Natural gas is defined as "...gas obtained from boreholes and wells and consisting primarily of hydrocarbons".[156] Accordingly, it is not

---

[148]   Petroleum Act 1969, s. 1(2).
[149]   Petroleum Act 1969, s. 15(1) ("continental shelf").
[150]   e.g. Petroleum Act 1969, sch. 1, s. 35.
[151]   Petroleum (Production and Drilling) Regulations 1969, s. 61(1)(a).
[152]   Petroleum Act 1969, s. 15(1) ("crude oil").
[153]   Petroleum (Production and Drilling) Regulations 1969, s. 61(1)(c).
[154]   Petroleum (Production and Drilling) Regulations 1969, s. 63(1) ("casing-head petroleum spirit").
[155]   Petroleum Act 1969, sch. 1, s. 35(b)(iii), Petroleum (Production and Drilling) Regulations 1969, s. 61(1)(b-c).
[156]   Petroleum Act 1969, s. 15(1) ("natural gas").

apparent from the legislation whether natural gas royalty may be charged on the raw or processed resource.

All Production/Volume

Royalty on crude and spirit is calculated as a percentage of the chargeable value of these resources produced from the relevant area in the relevant period.[157] The chargeable value of crude and spirit is a product of the "reduced quantity" of the produced crude and spirit and the appropriate price, subject to certain financial deductions.[158]

Not all produced resources will attract a royalty. In particular, the Regulations state that no royalty is due on the following resources, which are deducted from the quantity of crude and spirit produced in the relevant quarter and area to determine a "reduced quantity" on which royalty is payable:

(a)   any crude oil or casing-head petroleum spirit certified by the Director of Petroleum Resources to have been used by the licensee or lessee in the relevant quarter for the purpose of carrying on drilling and production operations, or pumping to storage and refineries, in Nigeria;

(b)   any crude oil or casing-head petroleum spirit certified by the Director of Petroleum Resources to have been injected or returned by the licensee or lessee into a formation in the relevant quarter; and

(c)   any reasonable pipeline or evaporating losses of crude oil or casing-head petroleum spirit approved by the Director of Petroleum Resources as having been incurred by the licensee or lessee in the relevant quarter;[159]

Royalty may be payable on natural gas that is extracted and sold.[160] Royalty is not payable on flare or waste gas appropriated by the government for its own use or any use approved by it.[161]

Value

The value of the crude and spirit for which royalty is charged is a product of the "reduced quantity" (described above) and the appropriate price, subject to certain financial deductions.[162] Under the regulation, the export price of crude and spirit is established by the Minister of Petroleum Resources as the price free on board at a Nigerian port of export for crude or spirit of the gravity and quality in question. If the crude or spirit is delivered to a Nigerian refinery, the price is approved by the Director of Petroleum Resources. The price should bear a reasonable relationship to established posted prices or to prices at international trading export centres:

---

[157]   Petroleum (Production and Drilling) Regulations 1969, s. 61(1)(a).
[158]   Petroleum (Production and Drilling) Regulations 1969, s. 61(3)(c-d).
[159]   Petroleum (Production and Drilling) Regulations 1969, s. 61(3)(b).
[160]   Petroleum Act 1969, sch. 1, s. 35(b)(iii), Petroleum (Production and Drilling) Regulations 1969, s. 61(1)(b-c).
[161]   Petroleum (Production and Drilling) Regulations 1969, s. 61(1)(b).
[162]   Petroleum (Production and Drilling) Regulations 1969, s. 61(3)(c-d).

61(4)   In this regulation "price", in relation to crude oil and casing head petroleum spirit, means the price free on board at a Nigerian port of export (or, in the case of crude oil or casing-head petroleum spirit delivered to a refinery in Nigeria, the price approved by the Director of Petroleum Resources at which the oil or spirit is delivered to the refinery) for oil and spirit of the gravity and quality in question, being a price which—

(a)   is from time to time established by the Minister as its price for Nigerian crude oil or Nigerian casing-head petroleum spirit, as the case may be, of that gravity and quality; and

(b)   bears a fair and reasonable relationship—

(i)   to the established posted prices of Nigerian crude oil or Nigerian casing-head petroleum spirit of comparable quality and gravity; or

(ii)   where there are no such established posted prices, to the posted prices at main international trading export centres for crude oil or casing-head petroleum spirit of comparable quality and gravity,

due regard being had in either case to freight differentials and all other relevant factors.[163]

Notably, the Regulations direct that the price should be established with due regard for freight differentials and "other relevant factors", but do not indicate what these might include.

The "chargeable value" of crude and spirit for royalty purposes is then determined by making certain financial deductions.   Under the Regulations, deductions are allowed for "…amounts of any costs approved by the Director of Petroleum Resources as having been properly incurred in respect of each such field by the licensee or lessee in handling, treating and storing that reduced quantity and in transporting it from the field to a tankship at a Nigerian port or to a refinery in Nigeria".[164]

The royalty rate is then applied to the "chargeable value" of the crude or spirit to determine the appropriate royalty payment.[165]   The royalty rates set in the Regulations depend on the volume of production and the depth of the water in which production occurs.   As production increases, the royalty rate also increases.[166] Further, as production moves to deeper water the royalty rate decreases.[167]

Site

Royalties are payable for resources produced from each field operated by the licensee or lessee in the "relevant area",[168] which is defined as the area affected by the licence or lease:

---

[163]   Petroleum (Production and Drilling) Regulations 1969, s. 61(4).
[164]   Petroleum (Production and Drilling) Regulations 1969, s. 61(3)(d).
[165]   Petroleum (Production and Drilling) Regulations 1969, s. 61(1)(a).
[166]   Petroleum (Production and Drilling) Regulations 1969, s. 62.
[167]   Petroleum (Production and Drilling) Regulations 1969, ss. 61(1)(a), 62.
[168]   Petroleum (Production and Drilling) Regulations 1969, s. 61.

"relevant area", in relation to an oil exploration licence, oil prospecting licence or oil mining lease, means the area affected by the licence or lease;[169]

Contributions in kind

The Regulations do not explicitly contemplate contributions in kind. Nonetheless, both the Petroleum Act and the Regulations state that certain gasses may be appropriated by the government for its own use.[170]

Annually

Royalty payments are due one month after the end of the quarter, including the quarter in which the licence or lease becomes effective.[171] A quarter is defined as a quarter of a calendar year.[172]

---

[169] Petroleum (Production and Drilling) Regulations 1969, s. 63(1) ("relevant area").
[170] Petroleum (Production and Drilling) Regulations 1969, s. 61(1)(b), Petroleum Act 1969, sch. 1, s. 35(b)(i).
[171] Petroleum (Production and Drilling) Regulations 1969, s. 61(1).
[172] Petroleum (Production and Drilling) Regulations 1969, s. 63(1).

CANADA (NEWFOUNDLAND AND LABRADOR)

Resource	Royalties in Newfoundland and Labrador are charged on "petroleum" which includes "oil" and "gas". "Oil" includes crude petroleum regardless of gravity produced at a well head in liquid form and any other hydrocarbons, except coal and gas, which may be extracted from deposits of oil sand, bitumen, bituminous sand, oil shale or from other types of deposits on the seabed or subsoil of the offshore area. There are no applicable regulations to determine royalties on "gas". Oil is deemed sold at the final point of measurement of the production facilities of a lease prior to the loading of oil for transportation, suggesting that crude oil is the relevant resource.
All Production/Volume	Royalties are not calculated on total production or total volume. Total production/volume is relevant in order to calculate the revenue of the interest holder on which royalties are charged. Revenue is calculated not only on the revenue from the total volume of oil sold but also on the volume of oil deemed sold. The volume of oil deemed sold includes the volume of oil transferred to the interest holder at the final point of measurement of the production facilities, with certain deductions based on factors such as a reduction in the volume of oil incidental to the transport of that oil. Royalty may be payable on test production.
Value	Newfoundland and Labrador charges only basic royalties where a producer's operations have not reached payout. Basic royalties are charged on the sum of gross revenue and the value of oil taken in kind by the Crown during that month, multiplied by the applicable royalty rate. "Gross revenue" is determined by calculating the "gross sales revenue" and deducting the applicable transportation costs incurred by an interest holder.
	Once a producer reaches payout, the producer becomes subject to Tier I and Tier II Incremental Royalties. Incremental royalty is charged on the product of the royalty rate and "net revenue", less the cumulative basic royalty and cumulative tiered incremental royalty paid by the interest holder. "Net revenue" is the sum of gross revenue, "incidental revenue" and the value of oil taken in kind, less applicable capital costs and operating costs for the relevant month (*i.e.* certain financial resources are deductible).
Contributions in kind	The Crown is permitted to take a royalty share or a portion of royalty in kind. The Minister of Natural Resources (the "Minister") must give at least six months written notice stating the month in which royalty share in kind will start and end being payable in kind. Where the Minister takes royalty in kind as a result of a default by the interest holder, the Minister must give at least five days' notice to the interest holder.
	Newfoundland and Labrador prescribes a formula to calculate the volume of oil the Minster can take in kind. The Minster has the authority to compel the relevant interest holder or other interest holders to store or transport oil received in kind on the Minister's behalf. The Minister is required to pay the interest holder for the provision of storage and transportation of oil that is taken in kind at the rates prescribed in the Royalty Regulations. Risk remains with the interest holder until the oil is delivered in the manner required by the government.

	CANADA (NEWFOUNDLAND AND LABRADOR)
Site	Basic royalty and tiered royalty are payable with respect to revenues from a particular lease. Each interest holder is responsible for assessment and payment of the royalty. "Interest holder" is the holder of that lease or share as recorded in the appropriate registry and there may be several "interest holders" in a particular lease.
Payments	Any reference to dollars, money or an amount of money shall be in Canadian currency.
Annually	Basic royalty and incremental royalty are due on the last day of the month following the month to which the royalty relates.

Introduction

The Newfoundland and Labrador offshore royalty regime is governed by the Petroleum and Natural Gas Act, RSNL 1990, c P-10[173] (the "Act") and the Royalty Regulations, 2003, NLR 71/03[174] (the "Royalty Regulations"). The government also sets individual royalty structures on a project-by-project basis.[175]

The Act prescribes that any "petroleum" produced under a "lease" is subject to payment of a royalty share to the Crown in an amount prescribed by the regulation.[176] "Petroleum" is defined to include oil and gas, in addition "to its ordinary meaning".[177] The Act does not specify the "ordinary meaning" of petroleum. In addition, Newfoundland and Labrador has not prescribed royalty regulations for natural gas and has regulations for offshore oil operations only.

"Lease" is defined by the Act to include a production licence issued by the Canada-Newfoundland and Labrador Offshore Petroleum Board.[178] Production licences are issued under the Canada-Newfoundland and Labrador Atlantic Accord Implementation Act (the "Accord Act").[179] Production licences, as per the Accord Act, are conferred with respect to the portions of the "offshore area" to which the licence applies.[180] "Offshore areas", as per the Accord Act, are defined as follows:

> *offshore area* means those submarine areas lying seaward of the low water mark of the province and extending, at any point, as far as

---

[173] Petroleum and Natural Gas Act, RSNL 1990, c P-10 ("Petroleum and Natural Gas Act").

[174] Royalty Regulations, 2003, NLR 71/03 ("Royalty Regulations").

[175] "Royalties and Benefits" *Department of Natural Resources* (28 July 2015), online: *Newfoundland and Labrador* <http://www.nr.gov.nl.ca/nr/royalties/index.html>; Petroleum and Natural Gas Act, s. 33.

[176] Petroleum and Natural Gas Act, s. 32.

[177] Petroleum and Natural Gas Act, s. 2(j).

[178] Petroleum and Natural Gas Act, s. 30(1)(c).

[179] Canada–Newfoundland and Labrador Atlantic Accord Implementation Act, SC 1987, c 3 (the "Accord Act"); the Province of Newfoundland and Labrador has mirror legislation at Canada-Newfoundland and Labrador Atlantic Accord Implementation Newfoundland and Labrador Act, RSNL 1990, c C-2.

[180] Accord Act, s. 80.

(i) a prescribed line, or

(ii) where no line is prescribed at that location, the outer edge of the continental margin or a distance of 200 nautical miles from the baselines from which the breadth of the territorial sea of Canada is measured, whichever is the greater;[181]

The Newfoundland and Labrador offshore royalty regime includes i) basic royalty; and ii) tiered incremental royalty.[182] Basic royalty is applicable to an interest holder in the period before payout (*i.e.* when revenues exceed costs) and is the sum of a) gross revenue and b) the value of oil taken in kind by the Crown, multiplied by the applicable basic royalty rate.[183] Incremental royalties are payable on net revenues less certain other royalties paid by the interest holder in the prior period.[184]

Resource

The Royalty Regulations, for the purpose of the determination of royalty share on offshore operations, only apply to "oil". "Oil" is defined in the Act as (i) crude petroleum regardless of gravity produced at a well head in liquid form and (ii) other hydrocarbons, except coal and gas, and hydrocarbons that may be extracted or recovered from deposits of oil sand, bitumen, bituminous sand, oil shale or from other types of deposits on the seabed or subsoil of the offshore area.[185]

The Accord Act vests title to petroleum produced during an extended formation flow test in an authorized person who conducts the test.[186] However, such title is conditional on compliance with the terms of the relevant authorization, approval or regulation, including the payment of royalties or other payment in lieu of royalties.[187] Royalties may be payable on oil produced during an extended formation flow test regardless of whether the authorized person has been granted a production licence. In addition, oil produced during an extended formation flow test will only be relevant for the calculation of royalties where the test provides significant information for determining "the best recovery system for a reservoir or for determining the limits of a reservoir or the productivity of a well producing petroleum from a reservoir and that does not adversely affect the ultimate recovery from a reservoir".[188]

All Production/Volume

The Newfoundland and Labrador regime charges royalties based on the revenue of the interest holder after allowing for various adjustments and incentives.

The production/volume of oil produced by an interest holder is a useful consideration in that it leads to the calculation of "gross revenue" (as applicable to "basic royalty" and "incremental royalty") and "net

---

[181] Accord Act, s. 2.
[182] Royalty Regulations, s. 4(2).
[183] Royalty Regulations, s. 6.
[184] Royalty Regulations, ss. 10(2), 11(2), 12.
[185] Petroleum and Natural Gas Act, s. 2(g).
[186] Accord Act, s. 140.2(1).
[187] Accord Act, s. 140.2(2).
[188] Accord Act, s. 140.2(3).

revenue" (as applicable to "incremental royalty").[189] "Gross revenue" is determined by calculating the "gross sales revenue" and deducting the eligible transportation costs incurred by an interest holder.[190] The Royalty Regulations prescribe the determination of "gross sales revenue" which is calculated by adding together the "revenue from sales of oil produced" by an interest holder and the "deemed sales of oil" by an interest holder, and allowing for the adjustment of any revenue from the sale of oil that had been included in calculations in the previous month.[191]

There are two ways in which the Royalty Regulations prescribe the calculation of "revenue from sales of oil produced". In the case of "arm's length transactions", "revenue from sales of oil produced" is calculated by multiplying the sale price of the oil with the quantity of oil sold.[192] In transactions that are not at arm's length, "revenue from sales of oil produced" is calculated by multiplying the quantity of oil sold with either the fair market value price set by the Minister of Natural Resources (the "Minister")[193] or by a "reference price committee".[194]

The Royalty Regulations prescribe "deemed sales of oil" by calculating the amount of oil transferred to the interest holder at the final point of measurement of the production facilities ("loading point") to be sold at the end of that month and such a quantity of oil is included in the calculation of the "gross sales revenue".[195] However, the Royalty Regulations allow reductions in the amount of oil deemed to be sold by exempting oil in inventory that was transferred to the interest holder within 91 days before the end of the month[196] or reductions for the "allowed shrinkage" using the appropriate measurement standards.[197] The "allowed shrinkage" is the reduction in the volume of oil incidental to the transport of that oil from the loading point directly to an entry valve at a transhipment facility in the province or the initial discharge point for that oil.[198] Allowed shrinkage is the lesser of (a) the actual shrinkage incurred; and (b) 0.2 per cent of the bill of lading net standard volume quantity of oil loaded at the loading point.[199] The quantity of such oil will not be deemed sold and therefore royalties will not be payable on such oil.

While basic royalties are applicable to any production by an interest holder, incremental royalties are only applicable when interest holders reach a certain payout. An interest holder reaches payout for "Tier I Incremental Royalty" and "Tier II Incremental Royalty" when its gross revenue and incidental revenue equals the sum of the relevant allowable deductions for tier specific allowances, basic royalty paid, and certain pre-development, capital, and operating costs.[200]

---

[189] Royalty Regulations, s. 7 and s. 12.
[190] Royalty Regulations, s. 7(1).
[191] Royalty Regulations, s. 7(2).
[192] Royalty Regulations, s. 7(3)(a).
[193] Royalty Regulations, s. 7(3)(b).
[194] Royalty Regulations, s. 7(3)(c).
[195] Royalty Regulations, s. 7(4).
[196] Royalty Regulations, s. 7(4)(a).
[197] Royalty Regulations, s. 7(4)(b).
[198] Royalty Regulations, s. 8(1).
[199] Royalty Regulations, s. 8(1).
[200] Royalty Regulations, ss. 10(3), 11(3).

Value

Before Payout

Before the operations of an interest holder reach a certain level of payout, the Newfoundland and Labrador Government charges only basic royalties. Basic royalties are charged on the sum of gross revenue and the value of oil taken in kind by the Crown during that month, multiplied by the applicable royalty rate.[201] The royalty rates that are in effect for leases issued after November 30, 2001, indicate that the basic royalty rate commences with the first month in which oil was produced under the lease.[202]

After Payout

After an interest holder reaches payout, the interest holder begins paying incremental royalty. The incremental royalty payable is equal to the royalty rate multiplied by "net revenue", less cumulative basic royalty and tiered incremental royalty paid by the interest holder for the period to the end of the previous month.[203]

"Net revenue" is the sum of gross revenue, "incidental revenue" and the value of oil taken in kind, less eligible capital costs and operating costs for the relevant month.[204] "Incidental revenue" includes consideration from the sale, lease, licence or other disposal or use of lease assets or technology under the lease where the cost was an eligible operating cost, eligible capital cost, eligible predevelopment, cost or a net decommissioning cost. Incidental revenue also includes certain proceeds received under insurance policies and certain adjustments to eligible capital costs and net decommissioning costs.[205]

Contribution in Kind

Section 34 of the Petroleum and Natural Gas Act permits the Crown to take a royalty share or a portion of royalty in kind. The Minister must give at least six months written notice stating the months in which the royalty share in kind will start and end being payable in kind.[206] Where the Minister intends to take in kind payment from an interest holder who is in default of its royalty share payment obligations under the Petroleum and Natural Gas Act, the Minister must give at least five days' notice to the interest holder.[207] In such a default situation, the Minister may also require another interest holder to store oil on behalf of the Crown, to prohibit delivery of oil to the defaulting interest holder, or to generally cooperate in the provision of lifting scheduling, transportation scheduling, and delivery plans.[208]

---

[201] Royalty Regulations, s. 6.
[202] Royalty Regulations, s. 90(1)(a).
[203] Royalty Regulations, ss. 10(2), 11(2).
[204] Royalty Regulations, s. 12.
[205] Royalty Regulations, s. 69.
[206] Royalty Regulations, s. 21(1).
[207] Royalty Regulations, s. 22(1).
[208] Royalty Regulations, s. 22(6).

The Royalty Regulations also prescribe two formulas for the calculation of the volume of oil that the Minister is entitled to take in kind with respect to royalty share that is payable to the Crown by an interest holder for a month. The first formula applies to the volume the Crown can take in kind before an interest holder attains Tier I payout while the second formula applies after an interest holder has attained Tier I payout. In the application of the formula, the calculation shall be made as if there has been no shrinkage in transit incurred by the interest holder whose royalty share is being taken in kind.

Volume before Tier I payout = $B [C + (A/R) - P] + [(U-T) /R]$

Volume after Tier I payout = $(B^p + I + U) / R$

The following is the list of definitions for the letters that form the formulas stated above.[209]

    (a) "volume" means the oil that the Crown is entitled to take in kind for the month;

    (b) "B" means the applicable basic royalty rate in effect under Part XIII or Part XIV;

    (c) "B^p " means the basic royalty payable for the month;

    (d) "I" means the incremental royalty payable for the month;

    (e) "C" means the volume of oil taken by the interest holder at the loading point during the month and includes oil taken in kind by the Crown with respect to that interest holder during that month;

    (f) "A" means the amount of payment received in advance by the interest holder for oil to be delivered after that month where that payment has not been accounted for in the calculation of royalty share in a previous month;

    (g) "R" means the price determined under subsection 7(9)[210] for the month in which oil is taken in kind or, for oil to which Part XIII applies, the price determined under subsection 81(1)[211] for the month in which oil is taken in kind;

    (h) "U" means a royalty share due in money and unpaid by an interest holder to the Crown when the Crown starts taking royalty share in kind;

    (i) "T" means the transportation and storage costs paid by the minister under subsection 29(3) for the transport of oil from the loading point to the place where the oil is transferred to the minister; and

    (j) "P" means the volume of oil transferred at the loading point under a lease to the interest holder for the month for which the interest holder received payment in a previous month and that payment was taken into account for calculation of the interest holder's royalty share in that previous month.

---

[209] Royalty Regulations, s. 23.
[210] The Minister shall determine a monthly price for oil in the month and that price shall be based upon the fair market value for oil during that month.
[211] Determination of the price of oil by the reference price committee on a monthly basis.

The in kind provisions of the Royalty Regulations also include provisions regarding the delivery of oil from the interest holder to the Crown, the obligations of the interest holder to the Minister, and the terms of lifting agreements between the Minister and the interest holder.

The Minister may require delivery of oil with respect to royalty share taken in kind at: (a) the final point of measurement of the production facilities of a lease prior to the loading of oil for transportation; (b) the point at which title has passed to an arm's length purchaser or when the oil enters the entry valve of a refinery or consuming facility; or (c) a transhipment facility.[212] As per the Royalty Regulations, delivery of oil to the Minister is considered to be completed where: (a) oil is delivered to a storage, transhipment or transportation facility as directed by the Minister; or (b) the Crown takes possession of that oil.[213] Oil that is taken from the interest holder remains at the risk of the interest holder until it is delivered as directed by the Minister.[214]

The Minister has an obligation to consult with all affected interest holders with respect to the delivery of oil in order to ensure transfer of that oil without significant disruption to the activities of the interest holders under the lease.[215] An interest holder's obligation to deliver royalty share in kind to the Minister will have priority over the interest holder's other obligations under contract with respect to the oil being taken in kind.[216] In addition, the Royalty Regulations also oblige the interest holder to take, transport, tranship and store the oil that is being taken in kind for the Crown as required by the Minister.[217] Where the Minister requires access to a transhipment facility or tanker for the storage or transportation of oil taken in kind, that access shall be supplied on terms that are customary for access by the interest holder, transhipment facility, or tanker.[218] The Minister shall pay the interest holder for the provision of storage and transportation of oil that is taken in kind at the rates prescribed in the Royalty Regulations.[219]

An interest holder may request that the Minister commences negotiations for a lifting agreement for royalty taken in kind.[220] The lifting agreement shall include terms and conditions of the delivery of oil to the Crown and the Royalty Regulations prescribe that the terms and conditions of the lifting agreement shall include the following:[221]

(a) the calculation of the volume of oil to be taken in kind at any one time;

(b) the delivery options of the Crown;

(c) the scheduling methodology to ensure that the minister has at least the same frequency of delivery that the interest holder from whom he or she is taking in kind would normally have;

---

[212] Royalty Regulations, s. 28(1).
[213] Royalty Regulations, s. 28(2).
[214] Royalty Regulations, s. 29(1).
[215] Royalty Regulations, s. 28(3).
[216] Royalty Regulations, s. 28(5).
[217] Royalty Regulations, s. 28(7).
[218] Royalty Regulations, s. 29(2).
[219] Royalty Regulations, s. 29(3).
[220] Royalty Regulations, s. 30(1).
[221] Royalty Regulations, s. 30(3).

(d) details respecting the satisfaction of the obligations under this Part of

> (i) the interest holder from whom the minister is taking in kind to lift, transport and store and deliver oil taken in kind by the Crown,
>
> (ii) the provision by other interest holders of access to lift, transport, store and deliver oil taken in kind to locations required by the minister, and
>
> (iii) the provision by other interest holders to provide access to and capacity to store oil taken in kind by the Crown at transshipment facilities.

The Royalty Regulations also prescribe that where a royalty lifting agreement cannot be concluded within 12 months after a request by the interest holder has been received by the Minster, either the Minister or the interest holder may refer the matter to arbitration.[222]

Site

In the Newfoundland and Labrador royalty regime, it is incumbent on each interest holder to be responsible for assessment and payment of the royalty share.[223] "Interest holder" is defined in subsection 3(1) of the Royalty Regulations, with respect to a lease or share in a lease, as the holder of that lease or share as recorded in the appropriate registry and there may be several "interest holders" in a particular lease.[224] Basic royalty and tiered royalty are payable with respect to revenues from a particular lease.[225]

An interest holder must not only pay royalties on the volume of oil sold for the relevant month but must also pay royalties for oil transferred to the interest holder at the "loading point".[226] Loading point means the final point of measurement of the production facilities of a lease prior to the loading of oil for transportation.[227]

For the purpose of calculating royalty share, oil shall be considered to have been "sold" prior to: a) when title to that oil passes to an arm's length purchaser; b) when the oil enters the entry valve of a refinery or consuming facility; or c) when the interest holder or an affiliate of that interest holder has received payment for the sale of that oil.[228]

Payments

The Royalty Regulations state that any reference to dollars, money or an amount of money shall be in Canadian currency.[229]

---

[222] Royalty Regulations, s. 30(4).
[223] Royalty Regulations, ss. 4-5.
[224] Royalty Regulations, s. 3(1)(k).
[225] Royalty Regulations, ss. 6, 10, 11.
[226] Royalty Regulations, s. 7(4)
[227] Royalty Regulations, s. 3(1)(l).
[228] Royalty Regulations, s. 7(8).
[229] Royalty Regulations, s. 3(3).

Where an amount is owed by an interest holder to the Crown, the Minister may recover the amount owed by setting-off the amount against an amount owed by the Crown to the interest holder.[230]

Annually

Basic royalty and incremental royalty are due on the last day of the month following the month to which the royalty relates.[231] To the extent that annual periods are relevant (*e.g.* with respect to certain reporting requirements,[232] reconciliation for royalty share payments,[233] and forecasting of annual royalty costs[234]), the calendar year is used.[235]

---

[230] Royalty Regulations, s. 4(7).
[231] Royalty Regulations, s. 5(1).
[232] Royalty Regulations, ss. 33-33.1.
[233] Royalty Regulations, s. 32.
[234] Royalty Regulations, s. 36.
[235] Royalty Regulations, s. 3(1)(n).

PART 2: TAX REGIMES

RUSSIAN FEDERATION

Resource	While resources will vary depending on the extraction process, they must meet certain standards. The particular extraction process is approved by the relevant licence/permit. The Tax Code distinguishes between the extraction process and further processing. Products of the processing industry (*e.g.* enrichment) are not "commercial minerals" that are taxed under the Tax Code. Dewatered, desalted, and stabilized oil is subject to taxation.
All Production/ Volume	If measurement is performed after the extraction process is complete, losses during extraction must be accounted for. However, certain permitted levels of losses are taxed at a zero rate. Certain reinjected gas, gasses that are associated with oil production, and hydrocarbon resources extracted from new offshore reservoirs may also be zero-rated.
Value	Commercial minerals may be valued based on the sale price excluding subsidies, value added tax, excise duties, and certain delivery expenses. If there is no sale, the resource value may be determined based on the expenses of production. The tax rate may be influenced by world oil prices, degree of difficulty of oil extraction, magnitude of reserves, levels of hydrocarbon depletion, and the region and extraction properties of oil.
Site	Site is defined in terms of "accounting units" as set out in the State Balance Sheet of Reserves, and the subsurface site that was granted to the taxpayer for use in accordance with the relevant legislation.
Payments	If sale price needs to be converted to domestic currency, the relevant date is the date of sale. Certain resources may be valued in a foreign currency, which must then be converted into the domestic currency. The average price of the resource and currency over the tax period are used to make the appropriate calculation.
Contributions in kind	-
Annually	The tax period is set monthly, not annually.

Introduction

The extraction of mineral and petroleum resources in Russia is taxed under Chapter 26 of the Tax Code of the Russian Federation (the "Tax Code").[236] The tax is referred to as the Mineral Extraction Tax, and applies to "commercial minerals", a term which is defined to include various hydrocarbons and metallic minerals.[237]

---

[236] For original Russian language Tax Code see Налоговый кодекс Российской Федерации (НК РФ), online: *Федеральная налоговая служба* <http://nalog.garant.ru/fns/nk/>; English translation available at Tax Code, online: *EY*

The tax applies to commercial minerals extracted in the territory of the Russian Federation at a subsurface site that was granted in accordance with the legislation of the Russian Federation.[238] Commercial minerals that are extracted from the subsurface outside the territory of the Russian Federation but in territories under the jurisdiction of the Russian Federation (or which are leased from foreign states or used on the basis of an international agreement) will be subject to the Tax Code as well.[239] The Tax Code sets out the registration requirements for those taxpayers involved in production in the continental shelf or exclusive economic zone:

> Taxpayers which carry out the extraction of commercial minerals on the continental shelf of the Russian Federation, in the exclusive economic zone of the Russian Federation and outside the territory of the Russian Federation, where such extraction is carried out in territories which are under the jurisdiction of the Russian Federation (or which are leased from foreign states or used on the basis of an international agreement) on a site of subsurface resources which has been granted to the taxpayer for use, must be registered as taxpayers of tax at the location of an organization or at the place of residence of a physical person.[240]

Tax Base

Depending on the resource in question, the tax base will be either the quantity or the value of the resource. The tax base for resources other than coal and hydrocarbons is the value of the extracted resource. For coal and most hydrocarbons, the tax base is the quantity of the resource that has been extracted. However, there are several exceptions. Notably, the tax base for certain "new" offshore hydrocarbon deposits in specific geographic locations is the value of the extracted resource.

Tax Base as Quantity

The Tax Code sets out instructions for determining the "quantity" of extracted commercial minerals in respect of which a company must make tax payments to the Russian Government.[241] The preferred way to determine the quantity is called the "direct method".[242] Under the direct method the taxpayer uses devices to directly measure the quantity of mineral after the extraction process has been completed. Since the measurement takes place after the extraction process has been completed, the Tax Code requires the taxpayer to determine the amount of the resource that has been lost during the extraction process.[243] Accordingly, all of the resource that is extracted from the subsurface is considered for the tax calculation, even if some of the resource has been lost.

<http://www.ey.com/Publication/vwLUAssets/EY-russian-tax-code-part-two-eng/$FILE/EY-russian-tax-code-part-two-eng.pdf>.

[237] Tax Code, art. 337(2).
[238] Tax Code, art. 336(1)(1).
[239] Tax Code, art. 336(1)(3).
[240] Tax Code, art. 335(2).
[241] Tax Code, art. 339.
[242] Tax Code, art. 339(2).
[243] Tax Code, art. 339(3).

In particular, the procedure for metering and loss calculation for oil is set out by the government outside of the Tax Code:

> The quantity of extracted dewatered, desalted and stabilized oil and actual losses occurring in the process of the extraction thereof shall be determined by a subsurface user in accordance with the procedure for the metering of oil which is approved by the Government of the Russian Federation.[244]

Tax Base as Value

The calculation of value depends on whether the resource has been sold. If there is no sale price on which to base value, it is necessary to determine value on the basis of the expenses required to produce the resource.

Value Based on Sale Price

Although this method of value calculation applies mostly to non-petroleum resources, it remains particularly informative for the purposes of interpreting Article 82. If the producer has sold the resource, the value of the resource is a product of the quantity of the mineral extracted and the value of a unit of the mineral.[245] The value of a unit is equal to the producer's receipts from the sale divided by the quantity of the mineral sold.[246]

Notably, the Tax Code directs the producer to make certain deductions from its receipts for the sale of resources. Receipts should not include any subsidies, value added tax, or excise duties.[247] Most notably for the purposes of interpreting Article 82, the Tax Code directs the producer to reduce its receipts by the value of delivery and transportation expenses.[248]

Value Based on Expenses

If there are no sales of the extracted resource, "value" will be determined using the expenses of production. The following types of expenses related to the extraction of resources may form the value of the resource[249] materials, labour, amortization of property, repair of fixed assets, development of natural resources, liquidation costs or write-offs for certain assets,[250] facilities restoration and maintenance,[251] insurance,[252] and certain other expenses. Notably, the Tax Code enables minimum values for

---

[244] Tax Code, art. 339(10); see also Tax Code, art. 339(9) for the rules for certain oil.
[245] Tax Code, arts. 340(2), 340(3).
[246] Tax Code, arts. 340(2), 340(3).
[247] Tax Code, art. 340.
[248] Tax Code, art. 340.
[249] Tax Code, art. 340(4).
[250] Tax Code, art. 265(8).
[251] Tax Code, art. 265(9).
[252] Tax Code, art. 263.

hydrocarbons extracted at new offshore deposits.[253] The minimum value depends on the price of the resource in world markets or domestic markets.[254]

Tax Rate[255]

If "value" is used as the tax base, the tax rate is expressed as a percentage of the value. The tax base of most metallic minerals is expressed as value, though the tax base of some new hydrocarbon deposits is also expressed in value. If "quantity" is used as the tax base, the tax rate is generally expressed as a price per mass. The tax base of most hydrocarbons is expressed in quantity. The applicable rate is distinct for different types of resources. Depending on the extracted resource, the tax rate is calculated as a base rate which is adjusted for various factors that will ultimately impact a producer's net revenue.

Most crude oil is taxed on the basis of "quantity". The quantity of crude oil is multiplied by a base rate, expressed in price per tonne, which may be adjusted for certain "extraction factors" including movements in world oil prices,[256] degree of difficulty of oil extraction,[257] magnitude of reserves,[258] levels of hydrocarbon depletion,[259] and the region and extraction properties of oil.[260]

Most natural gas and gas condensate are taxed on the basis of "quantity", not value. The base rate for natural gas and gas condensate may be adjusted for certain factors, including the degree of difficulty of extraction and transportation expenses.[261]

Zero-rated Resources

One of the most important aspects of the Tax Code with respect to interpreting Article 82 is the application of a tax rate of zero per cent to certain resources which effectively exempts these resources from tax payments. Notably, losses of minerals during extraction are zero-rated if the losses are within a normative level that is approved by the government.[262] However, losses that exceed the permitted amount are not zero-rated. In this respect, the system is similar to that in the United States where companies are not required to pay a royalty on avoidable losses.

Other resources that are zero-rated for tax purposes are "associated gas"[263] (which has been described as gas extracted via an oil well) certain natural fuel gas that is injected into a formation to maintain formation

---

[253]   Tax Code, art. 340.1.
[254]   Tax Code, art. 340.1(2).
[255]   Tax Code, art. 342.
[256]   Tax Code, arts. 342(2)(9), 342(3).
[257]   Tax Code, arts. 342(2)(9), 342.2, 342.5.
[258]   Tax Code, arts. 342(2)(9), 342.5(3).
[259]   Tax Code, arts. 342(2)(9), 342.5(2).
[260]   Tax Code, arts. 342(2)(9), 342.5(4).
[261]   Tax Code, arts. 342(2)(10), 342(2)(11).
[262]   Tax Code, art. 342(1)(1).
[263]   Tax Code, art. 342(1)(2). For description of "associated gas" see "Global Oil and Gas Tax Guide" (2015) at p. 515, online: *EY* < http://www.ey.com/Publication/vwLUAssets/EY-2015-Global-oil-and-gas-tax-guide/$FILE/EY-2015-Global-oil-and-gas-tax-guide.pdf>.

pressure for the extraction of gas condensate,[264] as well as hydrocarbons of certain types (*e.g.* super-viscous oil[265]) and petroleum from certain new offshore reservoirs.[266]

Annually

The relevant tax period is a calendar month.[267] A producer's obligation to make a tax declaration in this respect arises in the tax period in which the extraction of commercial minerals begins.[268] To the extent that annual timing is relevant, the legislation uses the calendar year, and not a separately timed fiscal year.[269] For example, the determination of a transportation coefficient used to adjust the tax rate for certain natural gas is done annually, beginning at the start of a calendar year.[270]

Site

Although the Tax Code uses the term "site", it does not define it. Instead, the site determination is set out in the licence for production granted by the Russian Federation, and is related to accounting units as set out in the State Balance Sheet of Reserves:

> Article 336   Object of Taxation
>
> 1. The object of taxation for tax on the extraction of commercial minerals (hereafter in this Chapter referred to as "tax"), unless otherwise stipulated by clause 2 of this Article, shall be:
>
>> 1) commercial minerals extracted from the subsurface in the territory of the Russian Federation at a subsurface site (including from a hydrocarbon reservoir) which was granted to the taxpayer for use in accordance with the legislation of the Russian Federation. For the purposes of this Chapter, a hydrocarbon reservoir shall be understood to mean an accounting unit of reserves of one of the types of commercial minerals referred to in subsection 3 of clause 2 of Article 337 of this Code (with the exception of associated gas) in the State balance sheet of reserves of commercial minerals at a particular subsurface site within which no other accounting units of reserves have been designated;[...][271]

Resource

Under the Tax Code, "commercial mineral" is the equivalent of the term "resource" as it is used in Article 82. A significant issue for the use of the term "resource" is whether it means raw or processed resources.

---

264   Tax Code, art. 342(1)(13).
265   Tax Code, art. 342(1)(9).
266   Tax Code, arts. 342(1)(20).
267   Tax Code, art. 341.
268   Tax Code, art. 345.
269   See, *e.g.,* Tax Code, arts. 342(1)(1), 342.4(9)(1), 342.4(9)(4), 345.1(1), 345.1(2).
270   Tax Code, art. 342.4(14).
271   Tax Code, art. 336.

Chapter 26 of the Tax Code provides a limit on the level of processing allowed for the material under which it can still be considered a "commercial mineral". On this point, the definition of extracted commercial mineral is instructive:

Article 337   Extracted Commercial Mineral

1. For the purposes of this Chapter, the commercial minerals referred to in clause 1 of Article 336 of this Code shall be referred to as "extracted commercial mineral". In this respect, a commercial mineral shall be deemed to be a product of the mining industry and quarry development (unless otherwise envisaged by clause 3 of this Article) which is contained in mineral raw materials (rock, liquid or other mixture) actually extracted (recovered) from the subsurface (waste, losses) and is the first in terms of its quality to conform to a national standard, a regional standard, an international standard or, in the absence of such standards for a particular extracted commercial mineral, a standard of an organization.

Products obtained from the further processing (enrichment, technological conversion) of a commercial mineral which are products of the processing industry may not be deemed to be a commercial mineral.[…][272]

The Tax Code provides guidance on how the point in the extraction cycle should be addressed when calculating tax payments:

Article 339   The Procedure for Determining the Quantity of an Extracted Commercial Mineral

[…]

7. For the purpose of determining the quantity of a commercial mineral extracted in a tax period, unless otherwise envisaged by clause 8 of this Article account shall be taken of the commercial mineral in relation to which the set of technological operations (processes) associated with the extraction (recovery) of the commercial mineral from the subsurface (waste, losses) has been completed in the tax period.

In this respect, where a commercial mineral deposit is developed in accordance with a licence (permit) for the extraction of a commercial mineral, account shall be taken of the entire set of technological operations (processes) which are envisaged by the technical project for the development of the commercial mineral deposit.

8. In the event that mineral raw materials are sold and (or) used before the set of technological operations (processes) envisaged by the technical project for the development of a commercial mineral deposit has been completed, the quantity of the commercial mineral extracted in the tax period shall be determined as the quantity of the commercial mineral contained in those mineral

---

[272]   Tax Code, art. 337.

raw materials which were sold and (or) used for own requirements in the tax period in question.[…][273]

Overall, the Russian tax scheme is flexible enough to take into account that resources may be in a variety of states when tax payments become applicable.

Payments

The Tax Code contemplates that payments may be made in foreign currencies, and provides instructions on currency conversion for resource sales. The relevant date for making the conversion is the date of sale:

> Article 340   The Procedure for the Valuation of Extracted Commercial Minerals for the Purpose of Determining the Tax Base
>
> […]
>
> 2. […] Where receipts from the sale of an extracted commercial mineral are received in a foreign currency, it shall be translated into roubles on the basis of the exchange rate established by the Central Bank of the Russian Federation as at the date on which the extracted commercial mineral is sold, which shall be defined depending on the method of recognising income which has been selected by the taxpayer in accordance with Article 271 or Article 273 of this Code. […][274]

The Tax Code also recognizes that certain resources may be valued in a foreign currency, which must then be converted into the domestic currency. The average price of the resource and of the currency over the tax period may be used to make the appropriate calculation:

> Article 340.1   Special Considerations Relating to the Determination of the Value of Hydrocarbons Extracted at a New Offshore Hydrocarbon Deposit
>
> […]
>
> 2. [...] The price of natural fuel gas in the case of export supplies shall be determined as the product of the average price for the tax period which has ended of natural fuel gas supplied beyond the boundaries of the customs territory of the Customs Union, expressed in US dollars per unit of natural fuel gas, and the average value for that tax period of the exchange rate of the US dollar to the Russian Federation rouble which is set by the Central Bank of the Russian Federation.
>
> [...]
>
> 4. The average value of the exchange rate of the US dollar to the Russian Federation rouble for a tax period shall be determined by a taxpayer independently as the arithmetic mean of the exchange rate of the US dollar to the Russian Federation rouble set by the Central Bank of the Russian Federation for all days in the relevant tax period.[275]

---

[273] Tax Code, art. 339.
[274] Tax Code, art. 340.
[275] Tax Code, art. 340.1.

UNITED KINGDOM

Resource	Crude oil is valued at the time it is sold or appropriated for refining. Refining can be distinguished from "initial treatment". Initial treatment includes the separation of oil and gas, the liquefying of gas for transportation, as well as other processes that enable the hydrocarbon to be safely stored, loaded into a tanker, or accepted by an oil refinery. Initial treatment does not include refining or deballasting.
All Production/Volume	Gas that is reinjected, flared, or lost during production is generally not taxed, nor is petroleum that has been appropriated for use for production purposes (*e.g.* drilling/production operations, pumping petroleum onshore, initial treatment).
Value	If the resource was sold at arm's length, its value generally corresponds to the sale price. If the resource was sold through a non-arm's length contract (*i.e.* to an affiliated company) the value will be calculated so as to approximate the market value of the resource. Transportation receives standardized treatment regardless of what transportation arrangements were actually made under a sale contract. If value is calculated, the value is based on assumptions on the distance of transportation and the level of initial treatment of the product, such that the actual initial treatment and the actual transportation costs incurred are not relied on when calculating market values.
Site	The geographical basis for taxation is an "oil field", which is defined on a geologic basis.
Payments	Profits or losses resulting from currency conversions are not taxed. The relevant date for calculating a currency conversion will typically be the date of delivery or appropriation of the product, since this is the date that tax becomes payable.
Contributions in kind	-
Annually	There are two chargeable tax periods per year, ending on December 31 and June 30. As a "half year" is defined as "a period of six months ending at the end of June or December", it can be argued that on this basis, a reference to "annually" in Article 82 should be interpreted as a calendar year.

Introduction

Instead of charging a royalty on production, the United Kingdom taxes profits earned from a variety of activities related to petroleum development. The United Kingdom ceased taking royalty in kind on

December 31, 1988, and abolished royalty payments on January 1, 2003.[276] Despite the fundamental differences in the regime for payments related to petroleum production, the United Kingdom has responded to many of the same conceptual challenges that exist for the interpretation of Article 82.

Several different taxes apply to resource producers that operate under the jurisdiction of the United Kingdom. One tax that is of particular interest for the interpretation of Article 82 is the Petroleum Revenue Tax ("PRT"), which is a tax on profits, not production. Under the PRT a producer is taxed on the difference between its receipts and expenses for each field. Expenses in this context are effectively the financial resources that go into offshore activities. While the PRT, governed primarily by the Oil Taxation Act 1975, c 22 (the "Oil Taxation Act"),[277] does not apply to fields that were approved after March 16, 1993, it continues to apply to fields that were approved before this date.[278] The United Kingdom's annual budget released on March 16, 2016, indicates that the PRT will be zero-rated retroactive to January 1, 2016.[279] While the tax will be effectively abolished, it will not be formally abolished through legislative repeal so that certain taxpayers may benefit from decommissioning relief available under the Oil Taxation Act.[280]

Petroleum Revenue Tax

Notably, offshore areas including the continental shelf may be subject to the PRT. This is because the Oil Taxation Act applies to licences granted under Part I of the Petroleum Act 1998, c 17, which itself enables Her Majesty to grant licences to explore for and develop certain petroleum resources on the continental shelf.[281]

One of the sources of profit that is taxed under the PRT is the "gross profit" from resource disposition.[282] Gross profit is conceptually similar to value, and accordingly may be instructive for understanding methods of value calculation applicable to Article 82.

Value

Three types of transactions that contribute to a taxpayer's gross profit which are relevant to interpreting the term "value" as used in Article 82 are the price received from the sale of hydrocarbons through arm's length contracts, the market value of hydrocarbons sold through non-arm's length contracts, and the market value of hydrocarbons that have been appropriated by a taxpayer but not disposed of.[283]

---

[276] "PRT: royalty – chargeable or allowable [OT05540]" Oil Taxation Manual (12 November 2014), online: HM Revenue & Customs <http://www.hmrc.gov.uk/manuals/otmanual/ot05540.htm>.

[277] Oil Taxation Act 1975, c 22, ("Oil Taxation Act").

[278] Finance Act 1993, c 34, s. 185.

[279] "Budget 2016 Policy Paper" (16 March 2016), online: HM Treasury < https://www.gov.uk/government/publications/budget-2016-documents/budget-2016>.

[280] Ibid, note 141.

[281] Oil Taxation Act, s. 1(1); Petroleum Act 1998, c 17, s. 3(2).

[282] Oil Taxation Act, ss. 2(3)-2(5).

[283] Oil Taxation Act, s. 2(5).

An important distinction made under the tax scheme in the United Kingdom is whether or not the sale of petroleum happens at arm's length. This reflects the reality that sales to and from affiliated companies may not reflect the true value of the product sold. The Oil Taxation Act states that to qualify as an arm's length contract, the price must be the sole consideration for the transaction, the terms of the sale cannot be affected by a commercial relationship, and the seller cannot have any interest in the resale of the product.[284]

Arm's Length Sales

If the "arm's length" requirements are met, then the sale price of the resource is used to calculate the payable tax.[285] However, there are certain aspects of the sale price that may have to be adjusted under the Oil Taxation Act. Under arm's length contracts, the sale becomes taxable when the petroleum is delivered to the buyer.[286] This can be distinguished from Article 82, where the triggering event is related to production.

Accordingly, transportation costs are a significant issue in determining the price connected with an arm's length contract. Under the Oil Taxation Act, transportation receives standardized treatment regardless of what transportation arrangements were actually made under the sale contract:

2   Assessable profits and allowable losses

[...]

(5A)   In any case where oil is disposed of in a sale at arm's length and the terms of the contract are such that the seller is required to transport the oil from a place on land in the United Kingdom for or another country, or from its place of extraction (where that is in the territorial sea of the United Kingdom or a designated area), for delivery at another place in or outside the United Kingdom or to meet some or all of the costs of or incidental to its transportation from and to such places then, for the purposes of this Part of this Act:

(a)   the price received or receivable for the oil shall be deemed to be that for which it would have been sold, and

(b)   the oil shall be deemed to be delivered at the time it would have been delivered,

if the terms of the contract did not require the seller to meet any such costs as are mentioned above but did require the oil to be delivered:

(i)   in the case of oil extracted in the United Kingdom, at the place of extraction; or

---

[284]   Oil Taxation Act, sch. 3, para. 1.
[285]   Oil Taxation Act, s. 2(5)(a).
[286] " PRT: computations - tax point [OT05016]" *Oil Taxation Manual* (12 November 2014), online: *HM Revenue & Customs* <http://www.hmrc.gov.uk/manuals/otmanual/ot05016.htm>.

(ii)   in the case of oil extracted from strata in the sea bed and subsoil of the territorial sea of the United Kingdom or, in the case of oil first landed in another country, at the place in that or any other country or of a designated area, at the place in the United Kingdom at which the seller could reasonably be expected to deliver it or, if there is more than one such place, the one nearest to the place of extraction. [...][287]

Appropriations and Non-Arm's Length Sales

When sales are not at arm's length or when petroleum is appropriated for refining purposes without being sold, the appropriate value for taxation must be calculated using a complex set of rules under the Oil Taxation Act. The goal of these rules is to determine the market value of the resource.[288]

The type of product being valued is one of the primary considerations when determining the value of non-arm's length transactions. There are different valuation mechanisms for two different categories of oil. The term "oil" is broadly defined under the Oil Taxation Act as "[...] any substance so won or capable of being so won other than methane gas won in the course of operations for making and keeping mines safe".[289]

The different categories of oil are not distinguished based on their physical properties. Instead, they are distinguished based on whether there is sufficient trading of the resource to provide for a daily market value.[290] Category 1[291] oils have daily market values, and include products such as Brent and Forties.[292] Category 2 oils do not have daily market values, and include products such as Gryphon, liquefied petroleum gasses and condensates.[293] It should also be noted that "light gases" have a distinct valuation mechanism under the Oil Taxation Act.[294]

To ensure consistency in valuation the statute sets out, for each type of product, the contract conditions that are assumed in order to determine the calculated value. For example, when determining the value of a non-arm's length transaction for Category 1 oil, the calculation is performed based on the following assumptions, whether or not they are in reality achieved. These assumptions include the distance of transportation and the level of initial treatment of the product:

---

[287]   Oil Taxation Act, s. 2.
[288]   Oil Taxation Act, sch. 3, para. 2.
[289]   Oil Taxation Act, s. 1(1).
[290]   "PRT: valuation of crude oils and products - general principles [OT05305]" *Oil Taxation Manual* (12 November 2014), online: *HM Revenue & Customs* <http://www.hmrc.gov.uk/manuals/otmanual/OT05305.htm>.
[291]   Oil Taxation Act, sch. 3, para. 2(1B).
[292]   "PRT: valuation of crude oils and products- category 1 oil introduction [OT05315]" *Oil Taxation Manual* (12 November 2014), online: *HM Revenue & Customs* <http://www.hmrc.gov.uk/manuals/otmanual/OT05315.htm>.
[293]   "PRT: valuation of crude oils and products - list of oils within category 2 [OT05343]" *Oil Taxation Manual* (12 November 2014), online: *HM Revenue & Customs* <http://www.hmrc.gov.uk/manuals/otmanual/OT05343.htm>.
[294]   Oil Taxation Act, sch. 3, para. 3A; "PRT: valuation of non-arms length disposals and appropriations - gas: contents [OT05360]" *Oil Taxation Manual* (12 November 2014), online: *HM Revenue & Customs* <http://www.hmrc.gov.uk/manuals/otmanual/OT05360.htm>.

2[...]

(2)   The market value of any particular quantity of Category 1 oil of any kind is the price for which that quantity of oil of that kind might reasonably have been expected to be sold under a contract of sale that meets the following conditions--

(a)   the contract is for the sale of the oil at arm's length to a willing buyer;

(b)   the contract is for delivery of a single standard cargo of the oil;

(c)   the contract specifies a period of three days within which loading of the oil is to take place and that period includes the notional delivery day for the actual oil;

(d)   the contract requires the oil to have been subjected to appropriate initial treatment before delivery;

(e)   the contract requires the oil to be delivered--

(i)   in the case of oil extracted in the United Kingdom, at the place of extraction; or

(ii)   in the case of oil extracted from strata in the sea bed and subsoil of the territorial sea of the United Kingdom or of a designated area, at the place in the United Kingdom or another country at which the seller could reasonably be expected to deliver it or, if there is more than one such place, the one nearest to the place of extraction.

The terms as to payment which are to be implied in the contract are those which are customarily contained in contracts for the sale at arm's length of oil of the kind in question.[295]

Accordingly, the actual initial treatment and the actual transportation costs incurred are not incorporated into the calculated value.[296]

Once the type of product is identified, a notional delivery day needs to be assigned to determine the appropriate market price. The legislation provides extensive guidance on how to choose the notional delivery day on which the petroleum should be valued.[297] Notably, certain taxpayers are large enough to elect whether to dispose of oil through an arm's length or non-arm's length contract, depending on what method results in a lower valuation for PRT purposes. The United Kingdom has modified its valuation legislation in response to this and other tax avoidance behaviours.[298]

---

[295]   Oil Taxation Act sch. 3, para. 2.

[296]   Contract assumptions for Category 2 oils are set out in Oil Taxation Act 1975, c 22, sch. 3, para. 2(2AA) and for light gasses at para. 3A(2).

[297]   Oil Taxation Act, sch. 3, para. 1A; "PRT: valuation of crude oils and products - notional delivery day for stock, deliveries and appropriations [OT05308]" *Oil Taxation Manual* (12 November 2014), online: *HM Revenue & Customs* <http://www.hmrc.gov.uk/manuals/otmanual/ot05308.htm>.

[298]   "PRT: computations – outline [OT05012]" *Oil Taxation Manual* (12 November 2014), online: *HM Revenue & Customs* <http://www.hmrc.gov.uk/manuals/otmanual/ot05012.htm>.

Resource, Volume, and All Production

Some petroleum produced from an individual field may be appropriated for refining by the taxpayer instead of being sold. However, not all appropriated petroleum is subject to the PRT. In particular, the legislation does not require the valuation of oil that has been appropriated for use for production purposes,[299] defined as follows:

> "production purposes", in relation to an oil field, means any of the following purposes, that is to say--
>
> (a) carrying on drilling or production operations within the field; or
>
> (b) in the case of oil won from the field that was so won from strata in the sea bed and subsoil of either the territorial sea of the United Kingdom or a designated area, pumping it to the place where it is first landed in the United Kingdom or to the place in the United Kingdom or another country at which the seller in a sale at arm's length could reasonably be expected to deliver it or, if there is more than one place at which he could reasonably be expected to deliver it, the one nearest to the place of extraction; or
>
> (c) the initial treatment of oil won from the field;[300]

Initial treatment includes the separation of oil and gas, the liquefying of gas for transportation, as well as other processes that enable the hydrocarbon to be safely stored, loaded into a tanker, or accepted by an oil refinery. Initial treatment does not include refining or deballasting.[301]

Although the calculation of profits depends on the disposition rather than the production of petroleum, the body tasked with administering tax payments has faced similar issues as are now being addressed in respect of the interpretation of Article 82. While there is no statutory provision that explicitly sets out how products that are lost or flared during production should be valued, Her Majesty's Revenue and Customs ("HMRC") has stated that the practice is to ignore this production for the purposes of PRT:

> There is a statutory anomaly for which a common-sense practice is adopted. It concerns oil that is lost or flared after having been won. If "disposed of" simply means "ended his possession of" then this oil would strictly enter stock under OTA75\S2(5)(d)(ii). If, on the other hand, its meaning is not so extensive then this oil would end up treated as stock under OTA75\S2(5)(d)(i). It could be argued however that the market value was nil. So in practice oil lost or flared is ignored.[302]

Similarly, HMRC has addressed how reinjected gas should be treated. Since reinjected gas is used for "production purposes", HMRC has stated that it is excluded for the calculation of tax:

---

[299] Oil Taxation Act, s. 12(1) ("relevantly appropriated"), s. 5A(5A).

[300] Oil Taxation Act, s. 12(1) ("production purposes").

[301] Oil Taxation Act, s. 12(1) ("initial treatment").

[302] "PRT: computation - stock and oil in transit [OT05150]" *Oil Taxation Manual* (12 November 2014), online: *HM Revenue & Customs* <http://www.hmrc.gov.uk/manuals/otmanual/ot05150.htm>.

[…] There is no disposal of the gas when reinjected and neither is there a relevant appropriation within the terms of OTA75\S2(5)(cb). This is because injection to enhance recovery is deemed to be 'for production purposes' and so gas won from the field and then reinjected is excluded from the definition of relevant appropriation by virtue of OTA75\S12(1). Thus no charge to PRT exists at the time of reinjection. It is only when the gas is produced from the field and disposed of or appropriated that a charge to PRT will arise.[303]

PRT is calculated field-by-field. Accordingly, charges may arise when gas produced from one field is injected into another field for production purposes.[304]

Site

The Oil Taxation Act does not use the term "site" as a basis for PRT. Instead, the basis for taxation is an "oil field",[305] which is defined on a geological basis. According to HMRC, the Department of Energy and Climate Change is responsible for defining the appropriate fields:

> A field determination sets the boundary that encompasses the maximum extent of the field. This is taken as the maximum extent of all hydrocarbons present within the geological structure(s) that constitutes the field. Fields are thus determined on the basis of geological criteria. An oil field is defined for tax purposes in Schedule 1 Oil Taxation Act 1975. For a hydrocarbon accumulation to be determined as a field it must be physically separated from any other accumulation that might be present. Occasionally fields may have a top and a base or overlie or abut one another.[306]

Annually

Under the Oil Taxation Act, there are two chargeable PRT periods per year ending on December 31 and June 30.[307] Since the Oil Taxation Act defines a "half year" as "a period of six months ending at the end of June or December",[308] it may be argued that a reference to "annually" in Article 82 should be interpreted as a calendar year. Despite the simplicity of defining the two chargeable periods per year, the administration for the payment of PRT is complex. For a chargeable period, the taxpayer is required to pay six monthly installments commencing in the second month of the next chargeable period.[309]

---

[303] "PRT: commingling - PRT treatment of re-injected gas [OT05635]" *Oil Taxation Manual* (12 November 2014), online: *HM Revenue & Customs* <http://www.hmrc.gov.uk/manuals/otmanual/OT05635.htm>.

[304] *Ibid.*

[305] Oil Taxation Act, ss. 1(2), 12 ("oil field"); Oil Taxation Act, sch. 1.

[306] "The DECC role in the UK North Sea: the field determination process [OT01007]" *Oil Taxation Manual* (12 November 2014), online: *HM Revenue & Customs* <http://www.hmrc.gov.uk/manuals/otmanual/ot01007.htm>.

[307] "PRT: overview of PRT – outline [OT03050]" *Oil Taxation Manual* (12 November 2014), online: *HM Revenue & Customs* <http://www.hmrc.gov.uk/manuals/otmanual/OT03050.htm>.

[308] Oil Taxation Act, ss.1(3)-1(4).

[309] Finance Act 1982, sch. 19, para. 2.

Payments

Currency conversion is an important consideration for the payment of PRT. As is stated by HMRC, the Oil Taxation Act does not provide guidance on currency conversion. However, since profits or losses resulting from currency conversions do not arise from "oil won", such amounts should not be taxed:

> The charge is of course levied in sterling. The international trade in oil is however carried on largely in dollars and therefore the price receivable and the market values of most crude oil, condensates and LPGs is initially denominated in that currency. Most gas (with the exception of that landed overseas) is denominated in sterling.
>
> In order to bring the receipts and values into charge to PRT it is therefore necessary to translate the foreign currency amounts into sterling and to do so without bringing in profits and losses in currency transactions as such items are clearly not profits from oil won. With the exception of the computation of nomination reconciliation (see below) the Oil Taxation Acts are silent on how this is to be achieved.[310]

HMRC goes on to state that the relevant date for performing a currency conversion will typically be the date of delivery or appropriation of the product, since this is the date that the tax becomes payable under the Oil Taxation Act. Nonetheless, HMRC may be willing to accept the date that the seller receives payment for the sale as the relevant date for the currency conversion:

> Each of the main components that make up the PRT gross profit defined in OTA75\S2(5) are brought into charge by reference to the delivery or appropriation. Thus the date of delivery is the date on which it is relevant to consider the sterling value of any foreign currency transactions.
>
> However it is also the case that the normal trading terms within the industry allow certain periods of credit before payments for deliveries actually become due. Thus the taxable proceeds from any transaction will not normally be received on the actual date of delivery. In recognition of this therefore LB Oil & Gas is content to accept that the date of payment can also be a determining factor in setting the relevant date for the purposes of the translation into sterling.
>
> The clear principle in either case is that the relevant conversion date is tied closely to the terms of the actual sale and delivery of the oil or, in the case of non-arm's length disposals and appropriations, where there may be no contracts as such, to the normal terms of delivery for the particular product concerned. Thus for crude oil for example the normal credit terms would suggest a date of payment of around 30 days after the delivery date.[311]

---

[310] "PRT: computation - currency translation – outline [OT05075]" *Oil Taxation Manual* (12 November 2014), online: *HM Revenue & Customs* <http://www.hmrc.gov.uk/manuals/otmanual/ot05075.htm>.

[311] *Ibid.*

NORWAY

Resource	A norm price is set for a particular "norm price point". Once the product passes the delivery point specified for the norm price, it becomes taxable.
All Production/Volume	N/A. Profits are taxed, not production. The activities that are covered by the special tax set out in the Petroleum Taxation Act are extraction, processing, and pipeline transportation of petroleum.
Value	Value for petroleum is assigned through a "norm price", which is set independently by the Petroleum Price Board. The "norm price" takes into consideration achieved and quoted prices for petroleum of the same or a corresponding type, adjustments for differences in quality, and transportation costs to the North Sea area or other relevant markets, delivery date, payment date and other terms and conditions, achieved and quoted prices for petroleum products, with necessary adjustment for refining, and other comparable prices or valuations which may be available.
Site	Profits from Norway's continental shelf are not taxed on a field-by-field basis. The shelf district taxed under the Petroleum Taxation Act is considered a single district.
Payments	Norm prices quoted in Norwegian kroner and US dollars.
Contributions in kind	-
Annually	Taxpayers use the calendar year as the financial year.

Introduction

Profits derived from petroleum activities on Norway's continental shelf are taxed primarily under the Petroleum Taxation Act (the "PTA").[312] The application of the PTA geographically extends to internal Norwegian waters, Norwegian territorial seas and the continental shelf, and certain other areas outside of Norwegian territory to the extent permitted by international law:

> Section 1. *Scope of the Act*
>
> This Act governs the taxation of exploration for and extraction of subsea petroleum deposits, and activities and work relating thereto, hereunder pipeline transportation of extracted petroleum:
>
> > (a)   in internal Norwegian waters, in Norwegian territorial seas and on the continental shelf;

---

[312] Act of 13 June 1975 No. 35 relating to the Taxation of Subsea Petroleum Deposits, etc. (the Petroleum Taxation Act). Last amended by Act of 21 June 2013 No. 66, online: *Norway* <https://www.regjeringen.no/en/topics/the-economy/taxes-and-duties/Act-of-13-June-1975-No-35-relating-to-th/id497635/> (English); Lov om skattlegging av undersjøiske petroleumsforekomster m.v. [petroleumsskatteloven] 13. juni 1975 nr. 35, online: *Lovdata* <https://lovdata.no/dokument/NL/lov/1975-06-13-35?q=Petroleumsskatteloven> (Norwegian) ("PTA").

(b) in adjacent seas, insofar as concerns petroleum deposits that reach beyond the median line in relation to another state, to the extent that the right to extraction thereof has been conferred upon Norway by agreement with such other state;

(c) outside the realm or the seas mentioned in a), insofar as concerns the landing of petroleum, and activities or work relating thereto, to the extent that the right of Norway to impose taxes on activities and work as mentioned is laid down by general public international law or by special agreement with a foreign state; and

(d) within the realm insofar as concerns the transportation of petroleum by pipeline from areas as mentioned in a), b) or c), as well as other activities at loading and unloading facilities as part of the extraction and pipeline transportation of such petroleum. [...]

By the continental shelf shall in this Act be meant the seabed and subsoil of the submarine areas that extend beyond the Norwegian territorial sea, throughout the natural prolongation of the Norwegian land territory to the outer edge of the continental margin, but no less than 200 nautical miles from the base lines from which the breadth of the territorial sea is measured, however not beyond the median line in relation to another state.[313]

Notably, the areas in Section 1 of the PTA form one offshore district, which is the geographic basis for taxation. Accordingly, the site or field of production is significantly less important for calculating the tax payable under the Norwegian regime, and is of limited use for interpreting Article 82:

Section 3. Special rules on the determination of wealth and income.

[...](d) The areas mentioned in Section 1 shall, subject to the exceptions laid down by this Act, be considered one district (the shelf district).[...][314]

Norway does not charge royalty on petroleum production. Instead, profits earned in Norway's shelf district are subject to the ordinary income tax.[315] Profits earned from certain statutorily defined activities related to petroleum production in the shelf district are subject to an additional special tax.[316] The activities that are covered by the special tax set out in the PTA are extraction, processing, and pipeline transportation of petroleum.[317] Generally, costs related to taxable activities may be deducted from receipts in order to calculate taxable income. The PTA gives extensive guidance on how to perform this calculation.[318]

Value

One of the components of taxable income is the "norm price" of the petroleum product, which can assist in interpreting the term "value" in Article 82. The norm prices for petroleum are set by Norway's Petroleum

---

[313] PTA, s. 1.
[314] PTA, s. 3.
[315] PTA, ss. 2, 5.
[316] PTA, s. 5.
[317] PTA, s. 5.
[318] PTA, s. 3.

Price Board, and are intended to correspond to the market price of the petroleum as if it was traded between independent parties.[319] The Petroleum Price Board usually sets norm prices retrospectively every quarter, with each day in the quarter receiving a specified price.[320]

The PTA states that the norm price will account for achieved and quoted prices for petroleum products, the quality of the product, transportation costs, delivery dates, payment dates, and level of product refinement:

> [...]The norm price shall correspond to the price at which petroleum could have been traded between independent parties in a free marked [sic]. By "independent parties" are meant purchasers and sellers who do not, between themselves, have such common interests that this could have influenced an agreed price. The valuation shall take into consideration, inter alia, achieved and quoted prices for petroleum of the same or a corresponding type, with necessary adjustment for differences in quality, transportation costs, etc., to the North Sea area or other relevant markets, delivery date, payment date and other terms and conditions, achieved and quoted prices for petroleum products, with necessary adjustment for refining, etc., and other comparable prices or valuations which may be available. It shall be taken into consideration whether these are agreements between associated companies or other agreements where special factors or other conditions must have influenced price determination. The norm price may be determined as a joint price for petroleum that is extracted during a specific period of time. The Ministry may lay down more detailed guidelines to be observed in determining the price, and may in each individual case decide that the established norm price shall not apply.[...][321]

The rules for governing the norm price for petroleum products are set out in the PTA,[322] the *Forskrift om fastsetting av normpriser*[323] ("Regulations on the fixing of norm prices") and the *Forskrift om bruk av normpris ved ligningsbehandlingen*[324] ("Regulations concerning the use of the norm price by tax assessment procedure").

Norway's Petroleum Price Board sets norm prices for various oil fields in Norwegian kroner and US dollars.[325] It should be noted that it is not possible for the Petroleum Price Board to set a norm price for all hydrocarbons. For example, there is no norm price for natural gas, which is valued at its achieved sales

---

[319] PTA, s. 4.

[320] Forskrift om fastsetting av normpriser, 25. juni 1976 nr. 5 §2, online: *Lovdata* < https://lovdata.no/dokument/SF/forskrift/1976-06-25-5?q=norm>. For norm prices see, "Petroleum Price Board and the norm prices" *Ministry of Petroleum and Energy* (2 July 2014), online: *Norway* < https://www.regjeringen.no/en/topics/energy/oil-and-gas/petroleum-price-board-and-the-norm-price/id661459/>.

[321] PTA, s. 4.

[322] PTA, s. 4.

[323] Forskrift om fastsetting av normpriser, 25. juni 1976 nr. 5 §2, online: *Lovdata* < https://lovdata.no/dokument/SF/forskrift/1976-06-25-5?q=norm>.

[324] Forskrift om bruk av normpris ved ligningsbehandlingen (Undersjøiske etroleumsforekomster m.v.), 17. desember 1976 nr. 7, online: *Lovdata* <https://lovdata.no/dokument/SF/forskrift/1976-12-17-7?q=normpriser>.

[325] "Petroleum Price Board and the norm prices" *Ministry of Petroleum and Energy* (2 July 2014), online: *Norway* <https://www.regjeringen.no/en/topics/energy/oil-and-gas/petroleum-price-board-and-the-norm-price/id661459/>.

price.[326]   Nonetheless, in circumstances where the Petroleum Price Board has set a norm price, the calculated "norm price" applies to the transaction even if a producer sells its product through an arm's length contract. This is distinguishable from the taxation scheme in the United Kingdom, which provides different mechanisms for the valuation of oil sold in arm's length contracts and non-arm's length contracts.

Resource

A norm price is set for a particular "norm price point". As is set out in the *Forskrift om bruk av normpris ved ligningsbehandlingen*, once the product passes the delivery point specified for the norm price, it becomes taxable.[327]

Annually

Taxpayers are directed to use the calendar year as their financial year.[328]

---

[326]   *Ibid.*
[327]   *Forskrift om bruk av normpris ved ligningsbehandlingen*, §2. See also, Jan B Jansen and Joachim M Bjerke, "Norwegian Petroleum Taxation" at p. 41, online: *Bugge, Arentz-Hansen & Rasmussen* <http://www.bahr.no/no/aktuelt/saker/_attachment/2869?_download=true&_ts=135436a4dc8>.
[328]   PTA, s. 8.

Summary Chart

COUNTRY:	**UNITED STATES OF AMERICA**
RESOURCE:	Lessee is required to put oil and gas in marketable condition at no cost to the government. There are no standards for valuing processed oil, but there are separate standards for the valuation of processed and unprocessed gas. Generally, quantity and quality of oil and unprocessed gas are determined at a point of royalty settlement approved by the responsible government authority. If processed gas is being valued, the quantity is determined by the net output of the processing plant.
ALL PRODUCTION/ VOLUME	Royalty is not payable on resources that are unavoidably lost or used on or for the benefit of the lease (which may include off-lease uses). Royalty is not payable for certain gas plant products that are reinjected into a reservoir or used to operate a processing plant. Likely no royalty on test production.
VALUE	Value depends on whether production is disposed of through an arm's length or non-arm's length contract, and for gas, whether it is processed or unprocessed. Under arm's length sales, value is generally equal to "gross proceeds" from the sale. Value for non-arm's length sales is calculated to approximate market value. Applicable deductions may include transportation and gas processing costs. There are no deductions for marketing or putting product in marketable condition. Adjustments for quality and location differentials may be appropriate if value is calculated using market prices, or is related to an exchange agreement.
CONTRIBUTION IN KIND	The royalty is to be paid in value unless the Office of Natural Resources Revenue requires payment in kind. Lessee is required to put royalty production into marketable condition at no cost to government. If lessee processes royalty gas or delivers royalty oil or gas at a point not on or adjacent to the lease, a processing or transportation deduction may be available. The "Royalty-in-Kind Programme" is now closed.
SITE	The USA has defined "site" as an individual lease for the purposes of Article 82. The lease defines the area for which royalties are payable, though regulations on royalty relief set out complex rules on determining the area for which royalty relief may be applicable. Depending on the type of lease, royalties may be suspended on the basis of geological fields, lease areas, project areas, or particular wells.
PAYMENT	Valuation in foreign currency is not contemplated
ANNUALLY	Royalty is payable monthly

COUNTRY:	BRAZIL
RESOURCE:	Royalty is payable on natural gas and crude oil, not the products that result from refining. Volume and quality of production are determined at a "production measurement point" defined in the applicable development plan.
ALL PRODUCTION/ VOLUME	Royalty is calculated using the "total production volume", which excludes reinjected natural gas, and reasonable quantities of natural gas flared for safety or other operational needs. Royalty is payable on other resources that are lost, flared, or used in execution of operations. Royalty is due for test production if it is used economically.
VALUE	Value is a product of the production volume and the reference price. Reference price is the higher of (1) the sale price at fair market value, or (2) a minimum price set by the National Agency of Petroleum. Where sale prices are used to calculate royalty, the sale price excludes tax and transportation.
CONTRIBUTION IN KIND	-
SITE	Royalty is payable by field, defined in geological terms.
PAYMENT	Payments are made in Brazilian currency. If conversion is required for a sale, use the monthly average of the official daily exchange rates for the purchase of foreign currency, set by the Central Bank of Brazil, for the month in which the sale occurred.
ANNUALLY	Royalty is payable monthly. Certain additional participation payments are payable quarterly, according to the calendar quarter.

COUNTRY:	CANADA (ALBERTA)
RESOURCE:	Royalty is paid on crude oil. Quantity of royalty is calculated at the place where the oil is first measured after it is recovered. Royalty standards are available for the valuation of processed gas. The royalty share of natural gas is determined at a "royalty calculation point". If the gas is unprocessed, this is generally tied to the point of delivery from the gathering system, or if processed gas is being considered, at the processing or reprocessing plant.
ALL PRODUCTION/ VOLUME	If there are any actions that will artificially reduce the royalty share owing to the Crown, the royalty will be calculated as if that action had not taken place. Generally, flared solution gas is exempt from royalty payments. Further, royalty is not payable on certain natural gas or residue gas consumed as a fuel in operations for gathering or processing natural gas. Royalty credits for reinjected gas may be available.
VALUE & CONTRIBUTION IN KIND	Regulations set out complex calculations for determining "royalty share", which is payable in kind unless otherwise indicated. Royalty rate is based on the price and quantity of the resource, and depending on the resource may be influenced by density (oil), depth of the well event, acid gas content (gas), geographic location of the well, or the length of time the well has been producing. Deductions may be allowed for the use of certain innovative technologies used to improve recovery.

Oil royalty is generally taken in kind and delivered to the Crown at the place where it is first measured after it is recovered. Gas royalty is generally taken in value instead of in kind. The reference price used to determine value may be deducted by transportation, gathering, and processing costs. |
SITE	The relevant site for payment is the "well event". Alternatively, if there is a unit agreement, the "unit" may be the relevant site.
PAYMENT	Regulations provide a mechanism to convert "royalty share" to a monetary payment, where appropriate. No currency conversion mechanism provided.
ANNUALLY	-

COUNTRY:	CANADA (NEWFOUNDLAND AND LABRADOR)
RESOURCE:	Royalty is charged on oil. "Oil" includes crude petroleum regardless of gravity produced at a well head in liquid form. There are no applicable regulations to determine royalties on "gas". Oil is deemed sold at the final point of measurement of the production facilities of a lease prior to the loading of oil for transportation, suggesting that crude oil is the relevant resource.
ALL PRODUCTION/ VOLUME	Royalties are not calculated on total production or total volume. Total production/volume is relevant in order to calculate the revenue of the interest holder on which royalties are charged. Revenue is calculated not only on the revenue from the total volume of oil sold but also on the volume of oil deemed sold. The volume of oil deemed sold includes the volume of oil transferred to the interest holder at the final point of measurement of the production facilities, with certain deductions based on factors such as a reduction in the volume of oil incidental to the transport of that oil. Royalty may be payable on test production.
VALUE	Newfoundland and Labrador charges only basic royalties where a producer's operations have not reached payout. Basic royalties are charged on the sum of gross revenue and the value of oil taken in kind by the Crown during that month, multiplied by the applicable royalty rate. "Gross revenue" is determined by calculating the "gross sales revenue" and deducting the eligible transportation costs incurred by an interest holder.

Once a producer reaches payout, the producer becomes subject to Tier I and Tier II Incremental Royalties. Incremental royalty is charged on the product of the royalty rate and "net revenue", less the cumulative basic royalty and cumulative tiered incremental royalty paid by the interest holder. "Net revenue" is the sum of gross revenue, "incidental revenue" and the value of oil taken in kind, less eligible capital costs and operating costs for the relevant month (i.e. certain financial resources are deductible). |
CONTRIBUTION IN KIND	The Crown is permitted to take a royalty share or a portion of royalty in kind, if appropriate notice is given. Newfoundland and Labrador prescribes a formula to calculate the volume of oil the Minster can take in kind. The Minster has the authority to compel the relevant interest holder or other interest holders to store or transport oil received in kind on the Minister's behalf. The Minister is required to pay the interest holder for the provision of storage and transportation of oil that is taken in kind at the rates prescribed in the Royalty Regulations. Risk remains with the interest holder until the oil is delivered in the manner required by the government.
SITE	Basic royalty and tiered royalty are payable with respect to revenues from a particular lease. Each interest holder is responsible for assessment and payment of the royalty. "Interest holder" is the holder of that lease or share as recorded in the appropriate registry and there may be several "interest holders" in a particular lease.
PAYMENT	Any reference to dollars, money or an amount of money shall be in Canadian currency.
ANNUALLY	Basic royalty and incremental royalty are due on the last day of the month following the month to which the royalty relates.

COUNTRY:	AUSTRALIA
RESOURCE:	Determined at wellhead.
ALL PRODUCTION/ VOLUME	Wellhead production minus certain petroleum that is unavoidably lost before the quantity of petroleum is measured, used for the purposes of operations related to exploration or recovery, flared or vented in connection with petroleum recovery operations, or returned to a natural reservoir.
VALUE	-
CONTRIBUTION IN KIND	-
SITE	Site for royalty payment is established by the permit area, lease area, or licence area. Relief is available for certain uneconomic wells.
PAYMENT	-
ANNUALLY	Royalty is payable monthly.

COUNTRY:	NIGERIA
RESOURCE:	Royalty is charged on crude oil, casing-head petroleum spirit, and natural gas. Crude oil ("crude") means oil in its natural state before it has been refined or treated (excluding water and other foreign substances). Casing-head petroleum spirit ("spirit") means liquid hydrocarbons which have been obtained from natural gas by natural separation or by any chemical or physical process, and have not been refined or otherwise treated.
ALL PRODUCTION/ VOLUME	The quantity of crude or spirit on which royalty is charged is the produced quantity less the following volumes: (1) crude or spirit used for the purpose of carrying on drilling and production operations, or pumping to storage and refineries; (2) crude or spirit that is injected or returned by the licensee or lessee into a formation in the relevant quarter; and (3) any reasonable pipeline or evaporating losses.
	Royalty may also be payable on natural gas sold by a licensee or lessee, not including certain flare or waste gas appropriated by the government for its own use or for any purpose approved by it.
VALUE	Value of crude and spirit for the purposes of royalty is a product of the reduced quantity and the appropriate price, subject to certain financial deductions. The price is set by the government and should bear a reasonable relationship to established posted prices or to prices at international trading export centres, and should have due regard for freight differentials and "other relevant factors". Deductions are permitted for the cost incurred in handling, treating, and storing the "reduced quantity" and in transporting the quantity of crude and spirit from the field to a tankship at a Nigerian port or to a refinery in Nigeria. The royalty on crude and spirit is a percentage of the resource value. The rate depends on the production volume and the depth of the water in which production takes place.
CONTRIBUTION IN KIND	-
SITE	Royalties are payable for resources produced from each field operated by the licensee or lessee in the "relevant area", which is defined as the area affected by the licence or lease.
PAYMENT	-
ANNUALLY	Royalty payments are due one month after the end of the quarter and a quarter is defined as a calendar quarter.

COUNTRY:	RUSSIAN FEDERATION
RESOURCE:	While resources will vary depending on the extraction process, they must meet certain standards. The particular extraction process is approved in the relevant licence/permit. The Tax Code distinguishes between the extraction process and further processing. Products of the processing industry (e.g. enrichment) are not "commercial minerals" that are taxed under the Tax Code. Dewatered, desalted, and stabilized oil is subject to taxation.
ALL PRODUCTION/ VOLUME	If measurement is performed after the extraction process is complete, losses during extraction must be accounted for. However, certain permitted levels of losses are taxed at a zero rate. Certain reinjected gas, gasses that are associated with oil production, and hydrocarbon resources extracted from new offshore reservoirs may also be zero-rated.
VALUE	Commercial minerals may be valued based on the sale price excluding subsidies, value added tax, excise duties, and certain delivery expenses. If there is no sale, the resource value may be determined based on the expenses of production. The tax rate may be influenced by world oil prices, degree of difficulty of oil extraction, magnitude of reserves, levels of hydrocarbon depletion, and the region and extraction properties of oil.
CONTRIBUTION IN KIND	-
SITE	Site is defined in terms of "accounting units" as set out in the State Balance Sheet of Reserves, and the subsurface site that was granted to the taxpayer for use in accordance with the relevant legislation.
PAYMENT	If sale price needs to be converted to domestic currency, the relevant date is the date of sale. Certain resources may be valued in a foreign currency, which must then be converted into the domestic currency. The average price of the resource and currency over the tax period are used to make the appropriate calculation.
ANNUALLY	The tax period is set monthly, not annually.

COUNTRY:	UNITED KINGDOM
RESOURCE:	Crude oil is valued at the time it is sold or appropriated for refining. Refining can be distinguished from "initial treatment". Initial treatment includes the separation of oil and gas, the liquefying of gas for transportation, as well as other processes that enable the hydrocarbon to be safely stored, loaded into a tanker, or accepted by an oil refinery. Initial treatment does not include refining or deballasting.
ALL PRODUCTION/ VOLUME	Gas that is reinjected, flared, or lost during production is generally not taxed, nor is petroleum that has been appropriated for use for production purposes (e.g. drilling/production operations, pumping petroleum onshore, initial treatment).
VALUE	If the resource is sold at arm's length, its value generally corresponds to the sale price. If the resource is sold through a non-arm's length contract (i.e. to an affiliated company) the value will be calculated so as to approximate the market value of the resource. Transportation receives standardized treatment regardless of what transportation arrangements are actually made under a sale contract. If value is calculated, the value is based on assumptions on the distance of transportation and the level of initial treatment of the product, such that the actual initial treatment and the actual transportation costs incurred are not relied on when calculating market values.
CONTRIBUTION IN KIND	-
SITE	The geographical basis for taxation is an "oil field", which is defined on a geological basis.
PAYMENT	Profits or losses resulting from currency conversions are not taxed. The relevant date for calculating a currency conversion will typically be the date of delivery or appropriation of the product, since this is the date that tax becomes payable.
ANNUALLY	There are two chargeable tax periods per year, ending on December 31 and June 30. As a "half year" is defined as "a period of six months ending at the end of June or December", it can be argued that on this basis, a reference to "annually" in Article 82 should be interpreted as a calendar year.

COUNTRY:	NORWAY
RESOURCE:	A "norm price" for products is set for a particular "norm price point". Once the product passes the delivery point specified for the norm price, it becomes taxable.
ALL PRODUCTION/ VOLUME	Profits are taxed, not production. The activities that are covered by the special tax set out in the Petroleum Taxation Act are extraction, processing, and pipeline transportation of petroleum.
VALUE	Value for petroleum is assigned through a "norm price", which is set independently by the Petroleum Price Board. The "norm price" takes into consideration achieved and quoted prices for petroleum of the same or a corresponding type, adjustments for differences in quality, and transportation costs to the North Sea area or other relevant markets, delivery date, payment date and other terms and conditions, achieved and quoted prices for petroleum products, with necessary adjustment for refining, and other comparable prices or valuations which may be available.
CONTRIBUTION IN KIND	-
SITE	Profits from Norway's continental shelf are not taxed on a field-by-field basis. The shelf district taxed under the Petroleum Taxation Act is considered a single district.
PAYMENT	Norm prices quoted in Norwegian kroner and US dollars.
ANNUALLY	Taxpayers use the calendar year as the financial year.